I0478934

BLACK HISTORY FIGURES
Coloring Book

Famous Black People

Adult Coloring Books

Aryla Publishing 2019

978-1-912675-31-9

www.arylapublishing.com

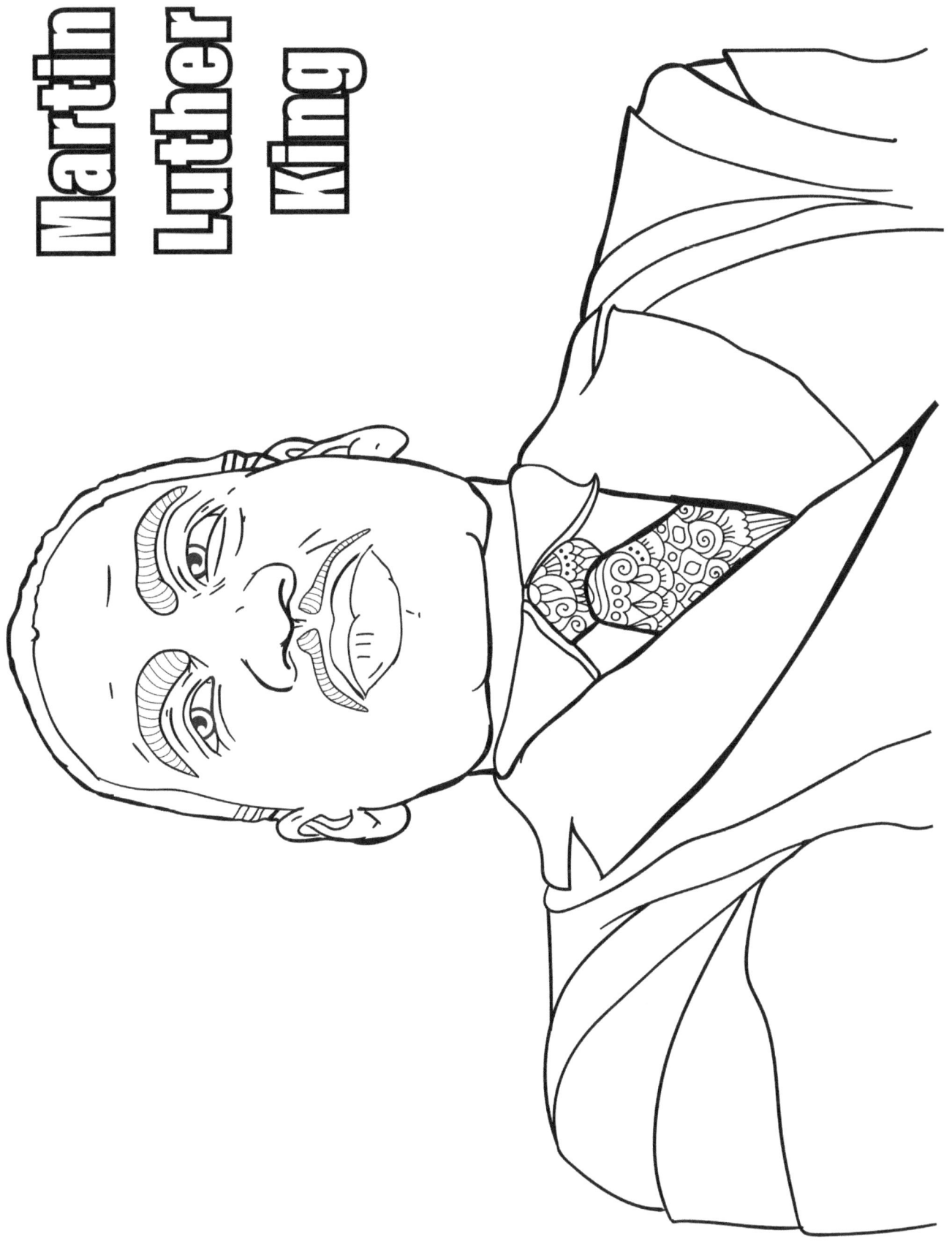

Martin Luther King

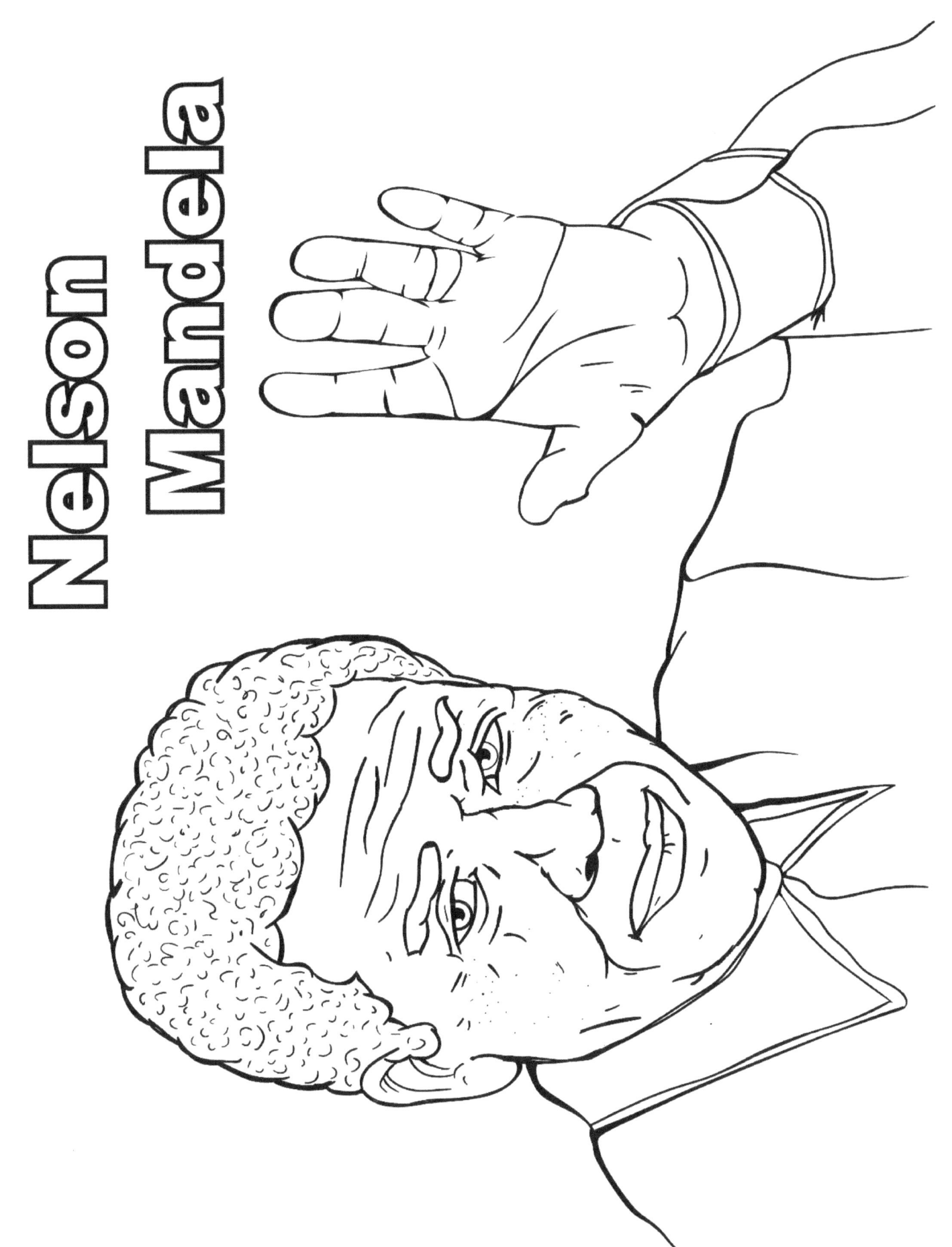

Nelson Mandela

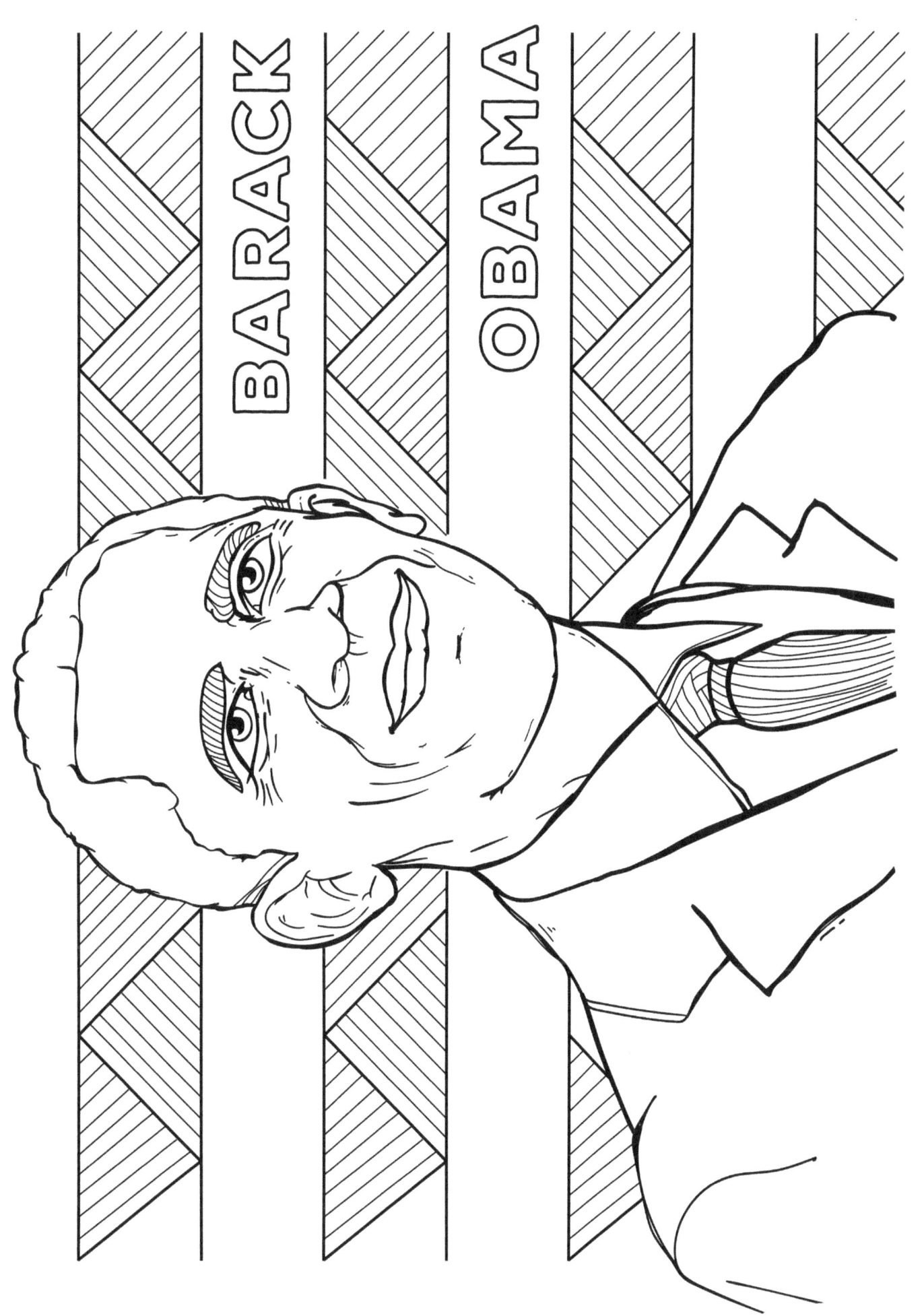

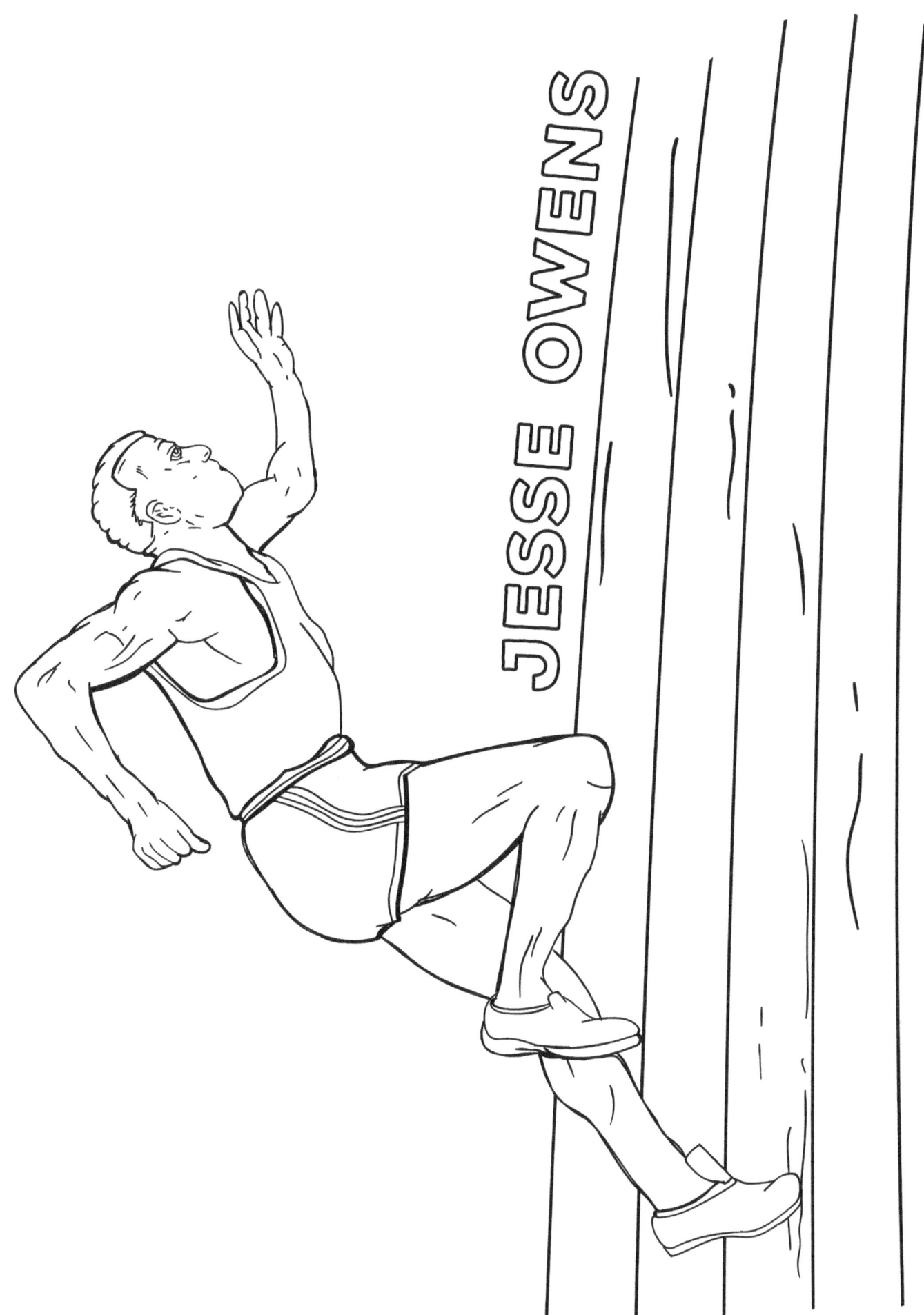

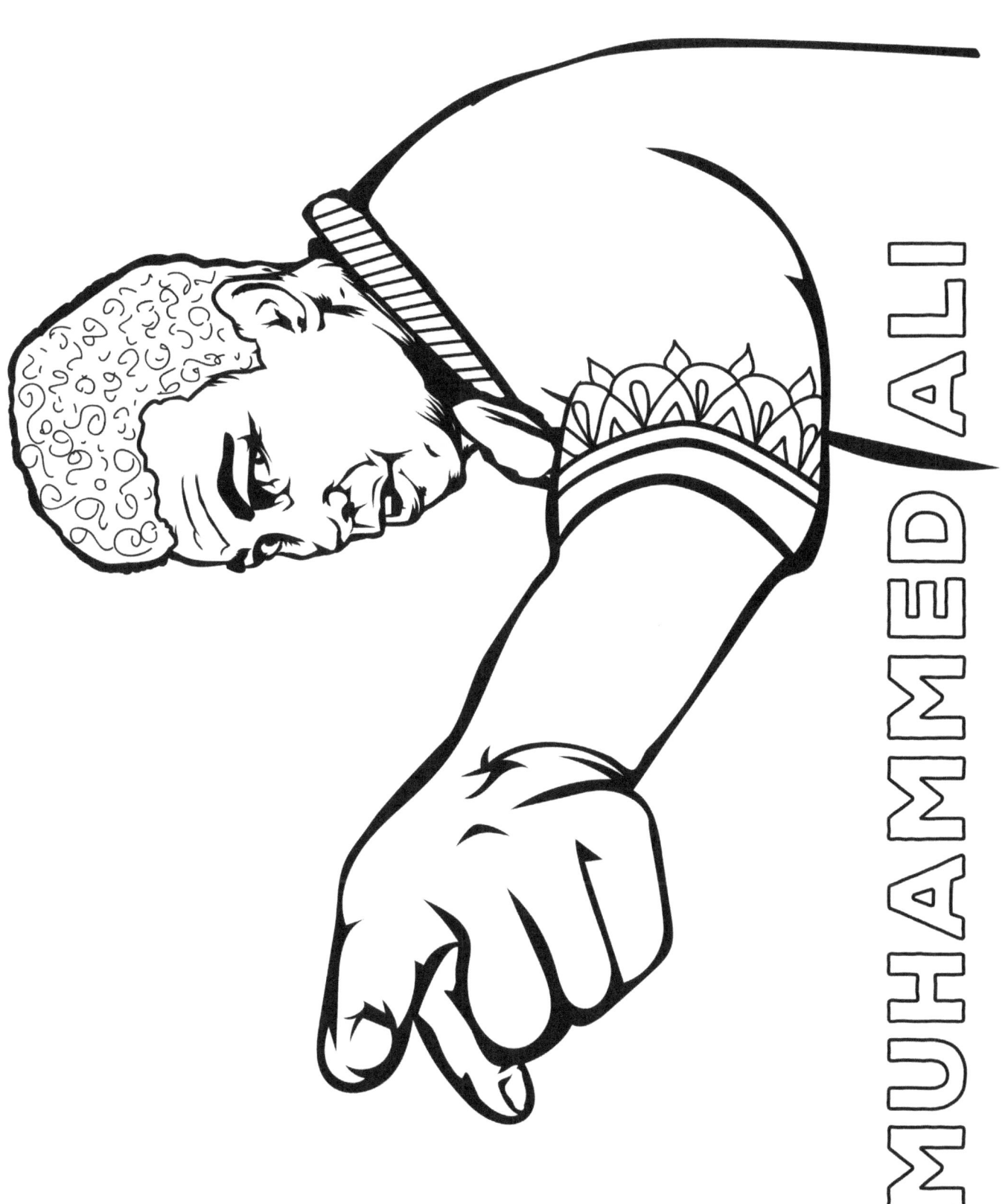

MUHAMMED ALI

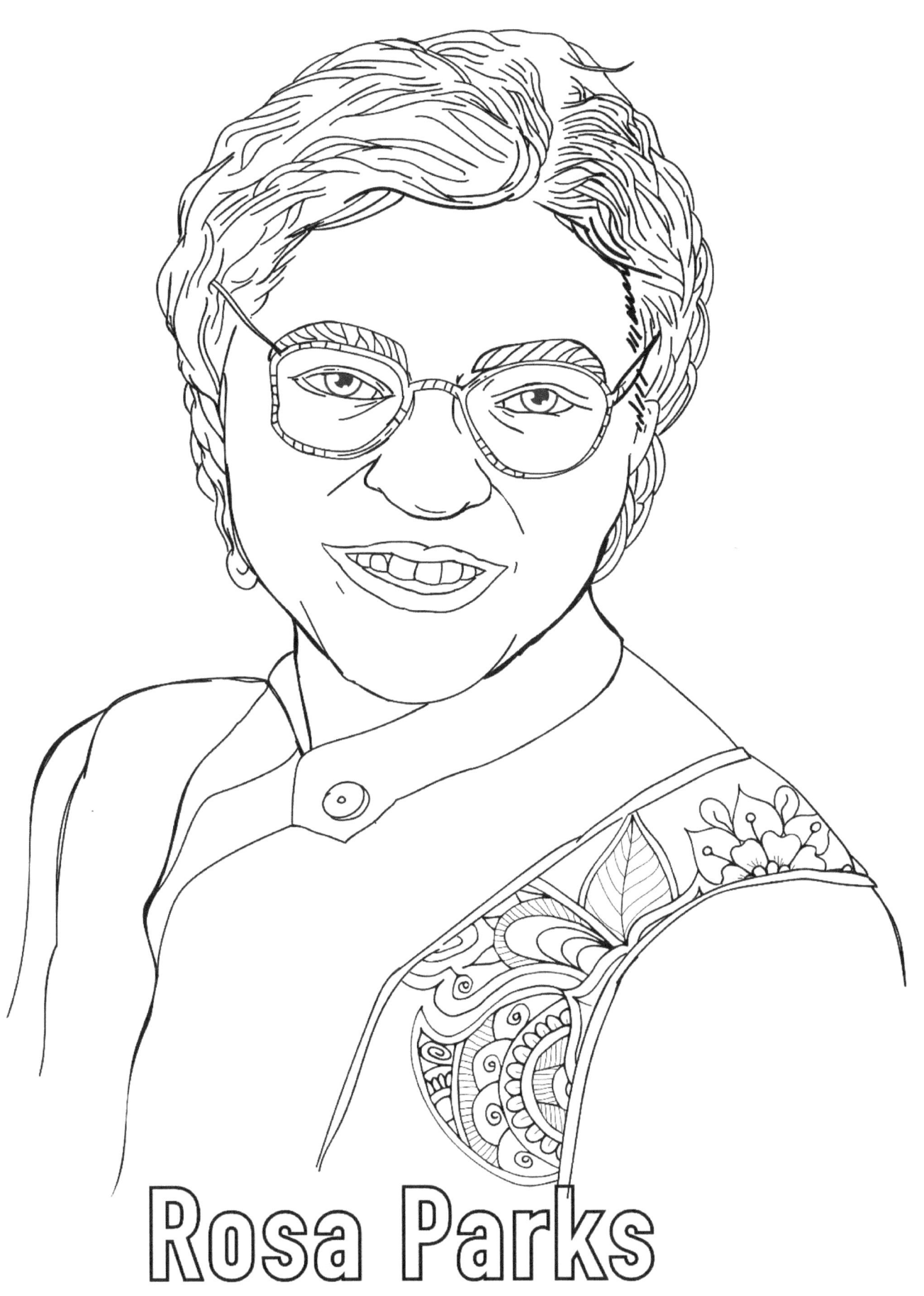

Rosa Parks

FREDERICK DOUGLASS

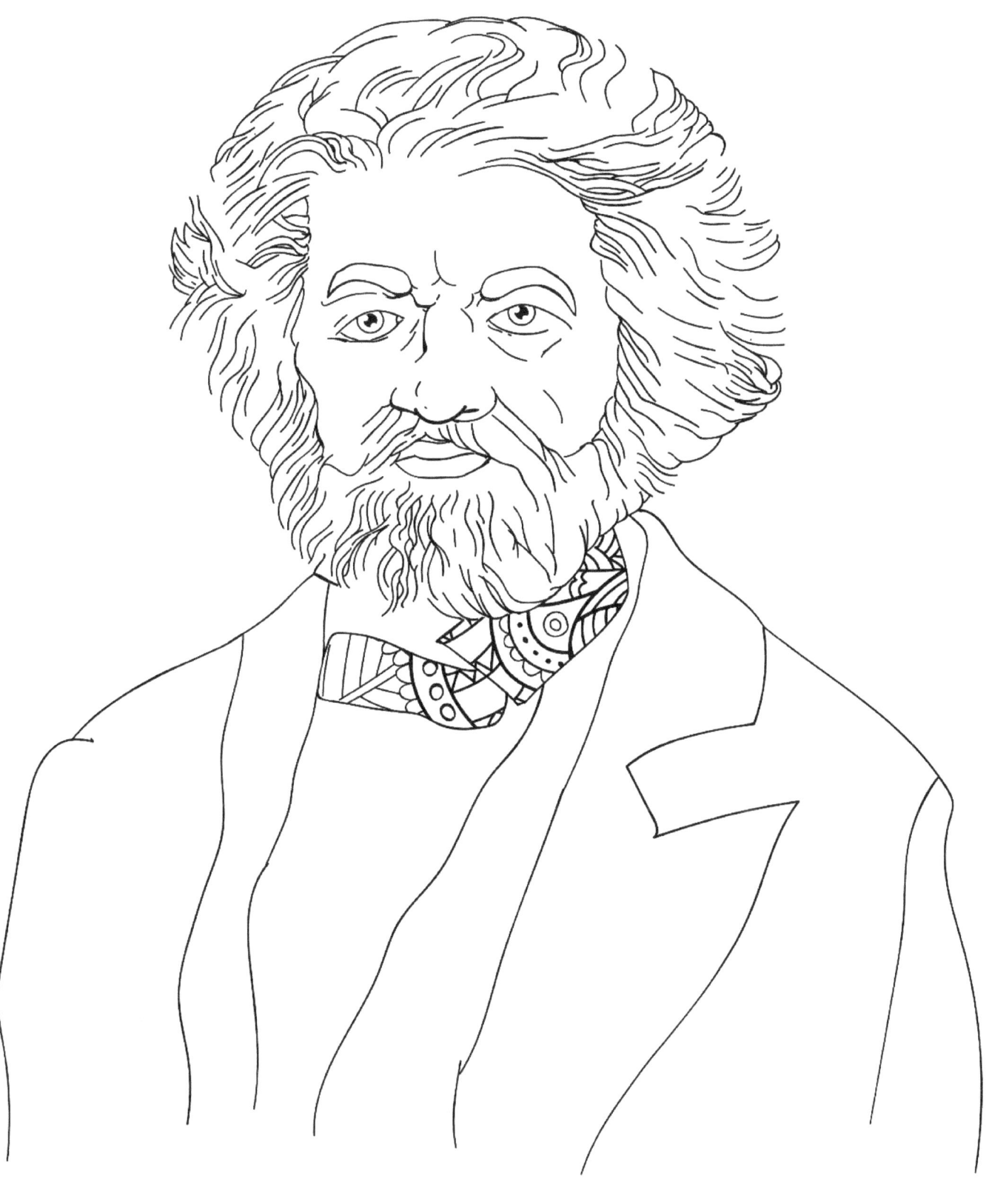

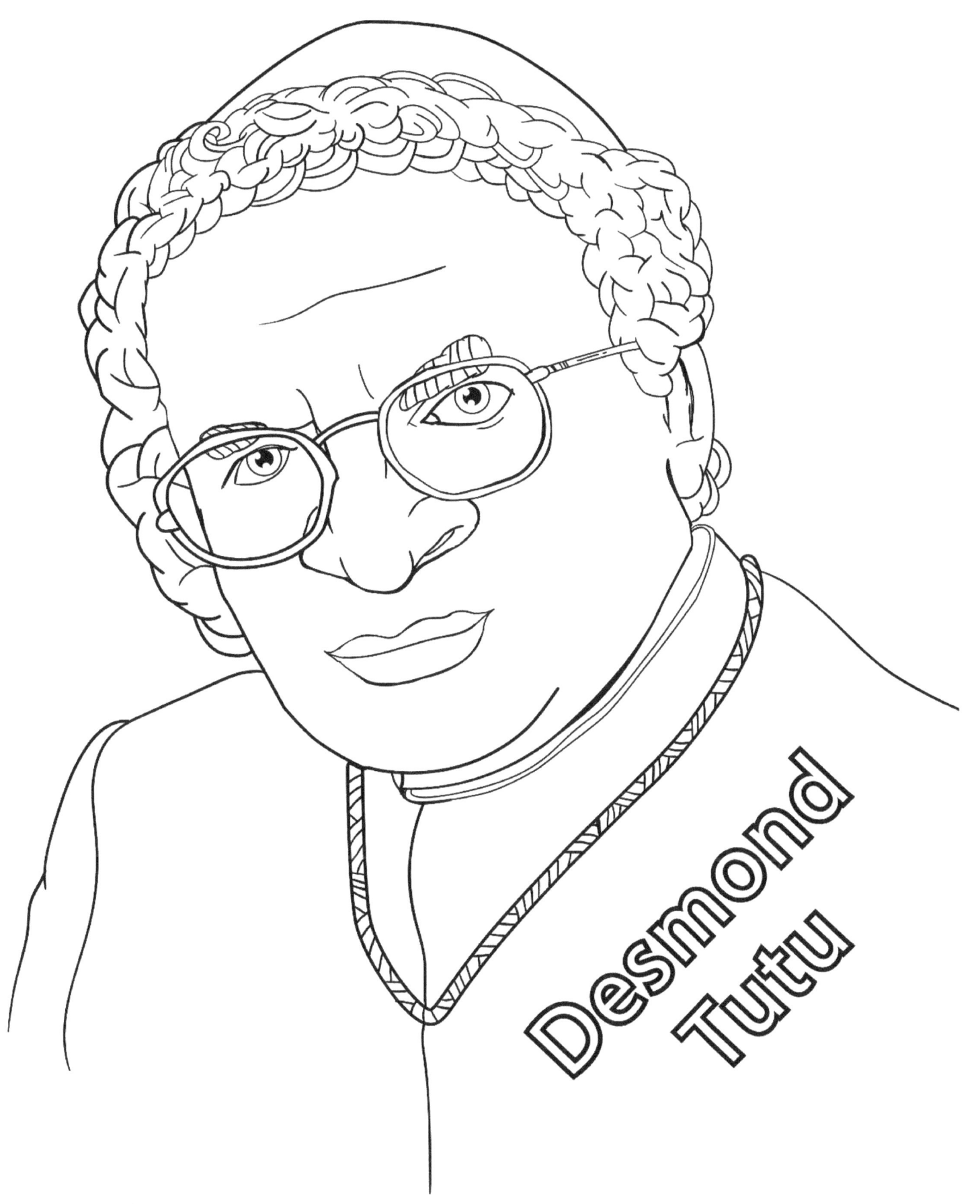

Desmond Tutu

BOB MARLEY

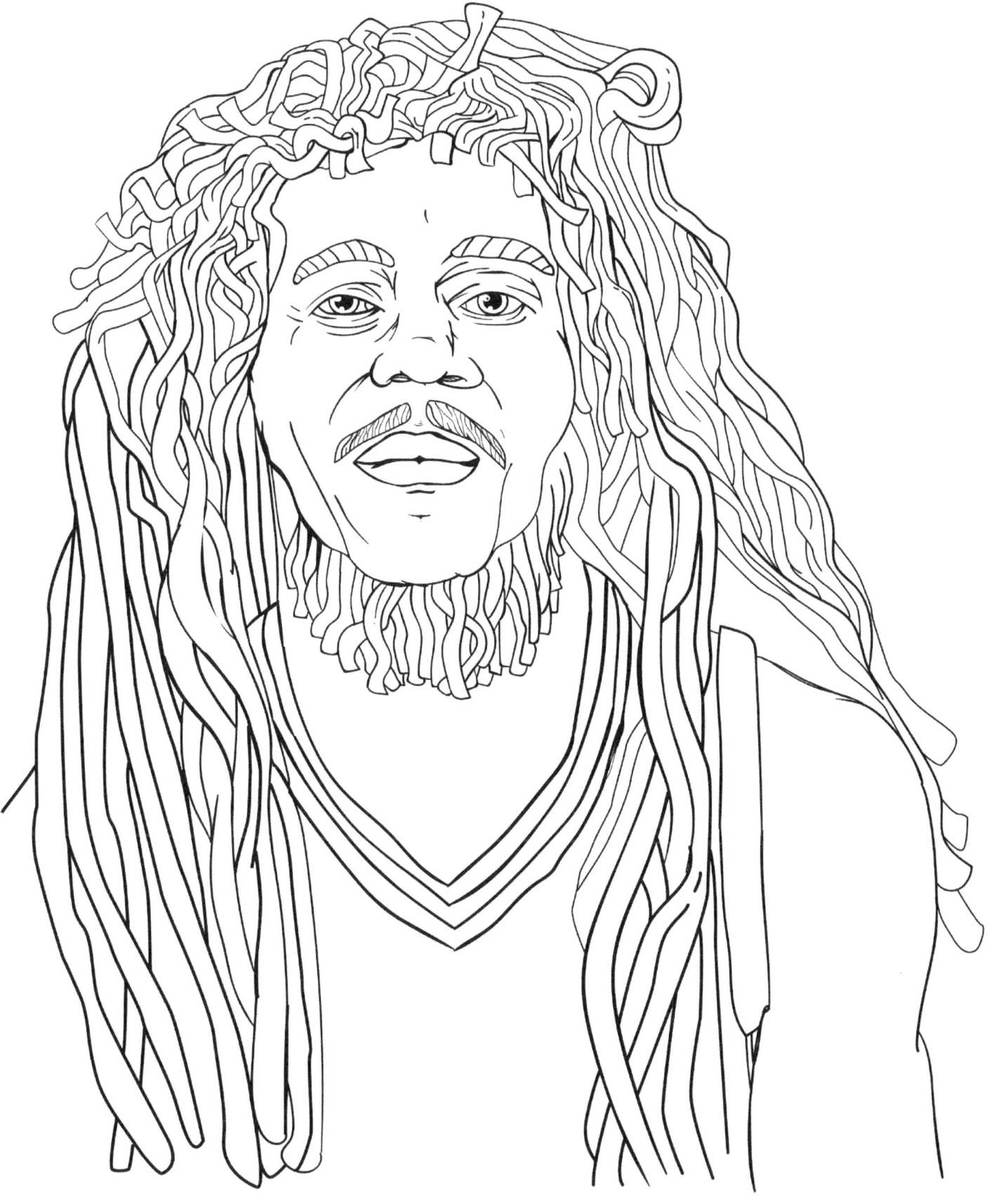

OPRAH WINFREY

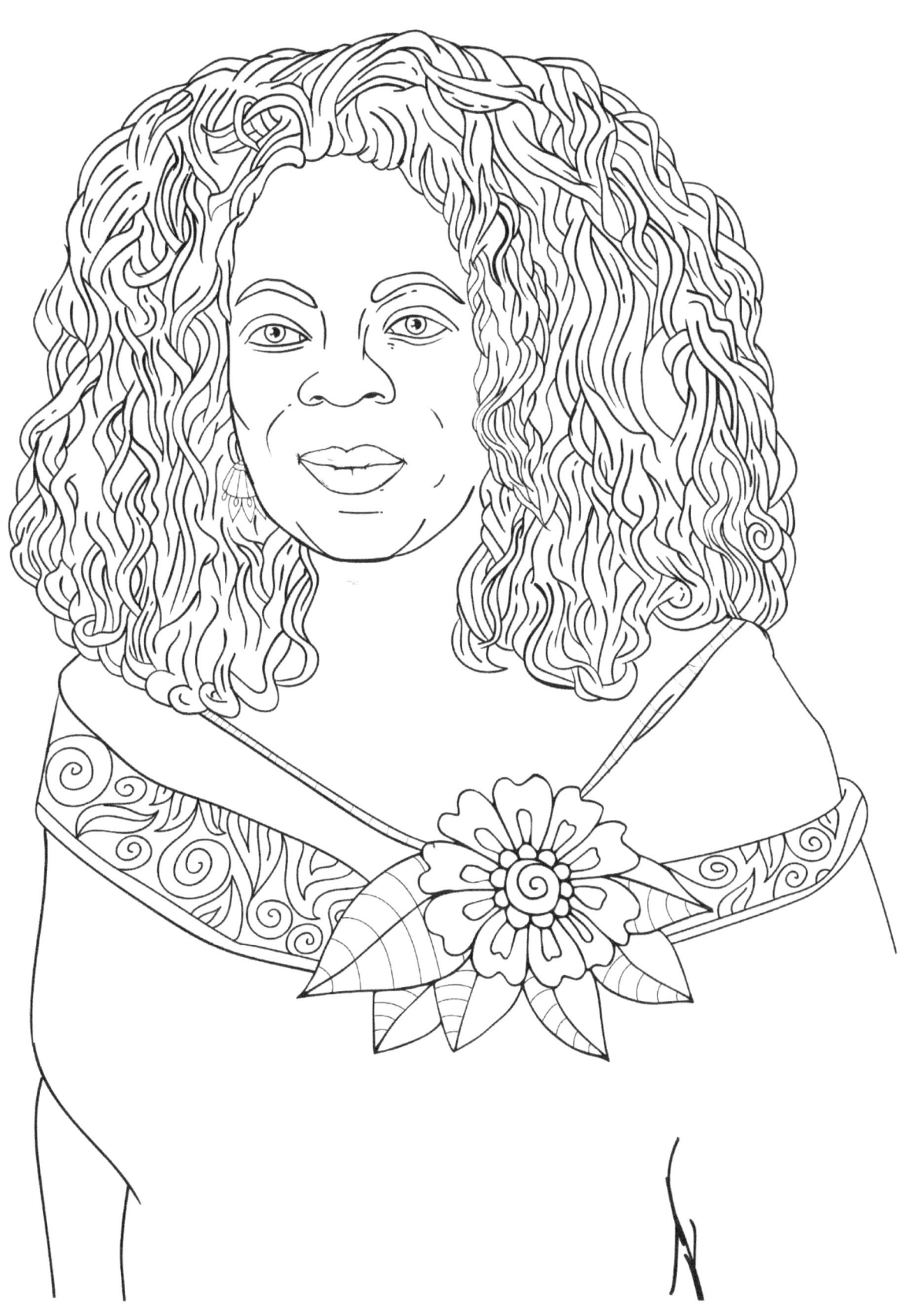

MAYA ANGELOU

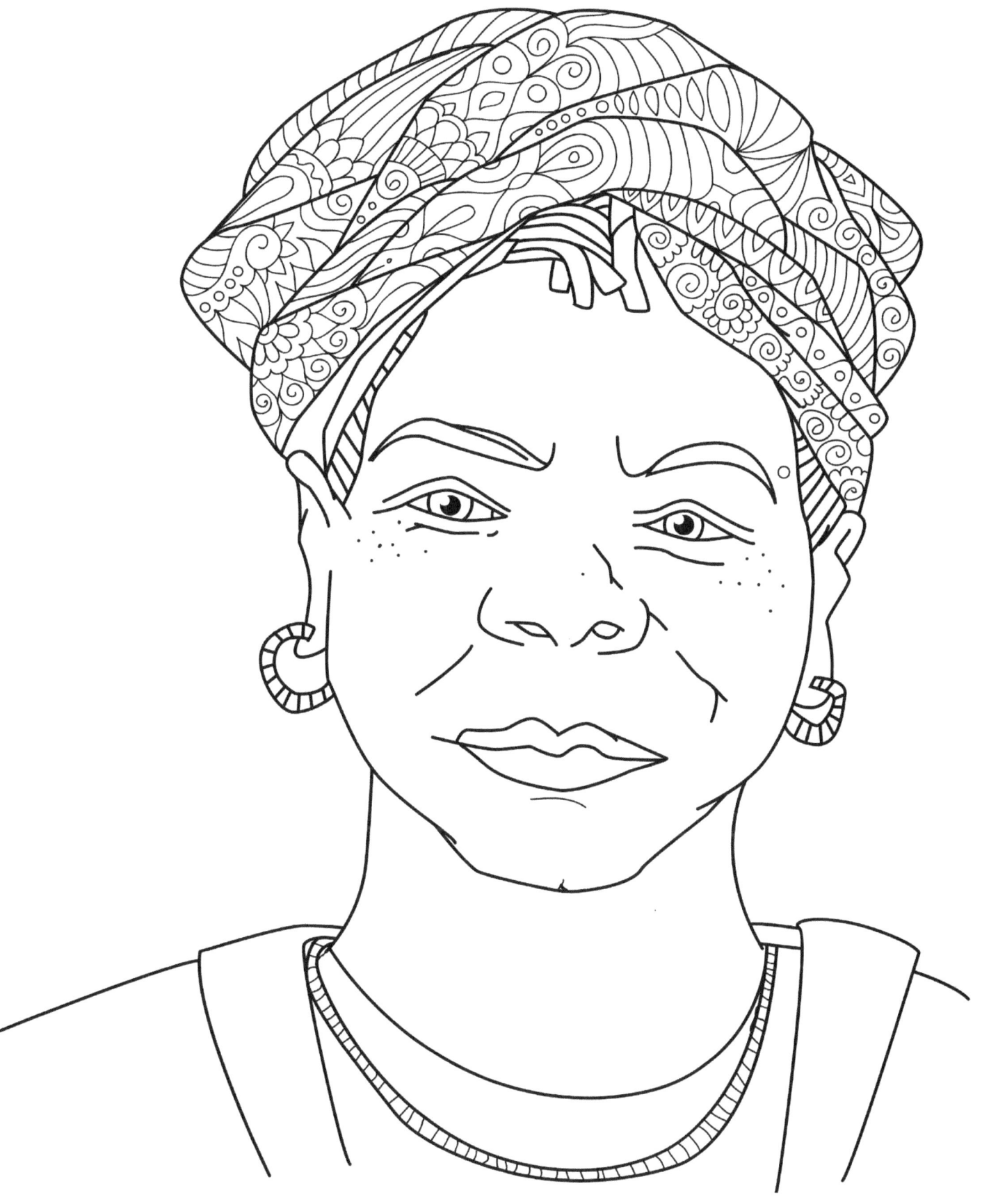

NANNY OF THE MAROONS

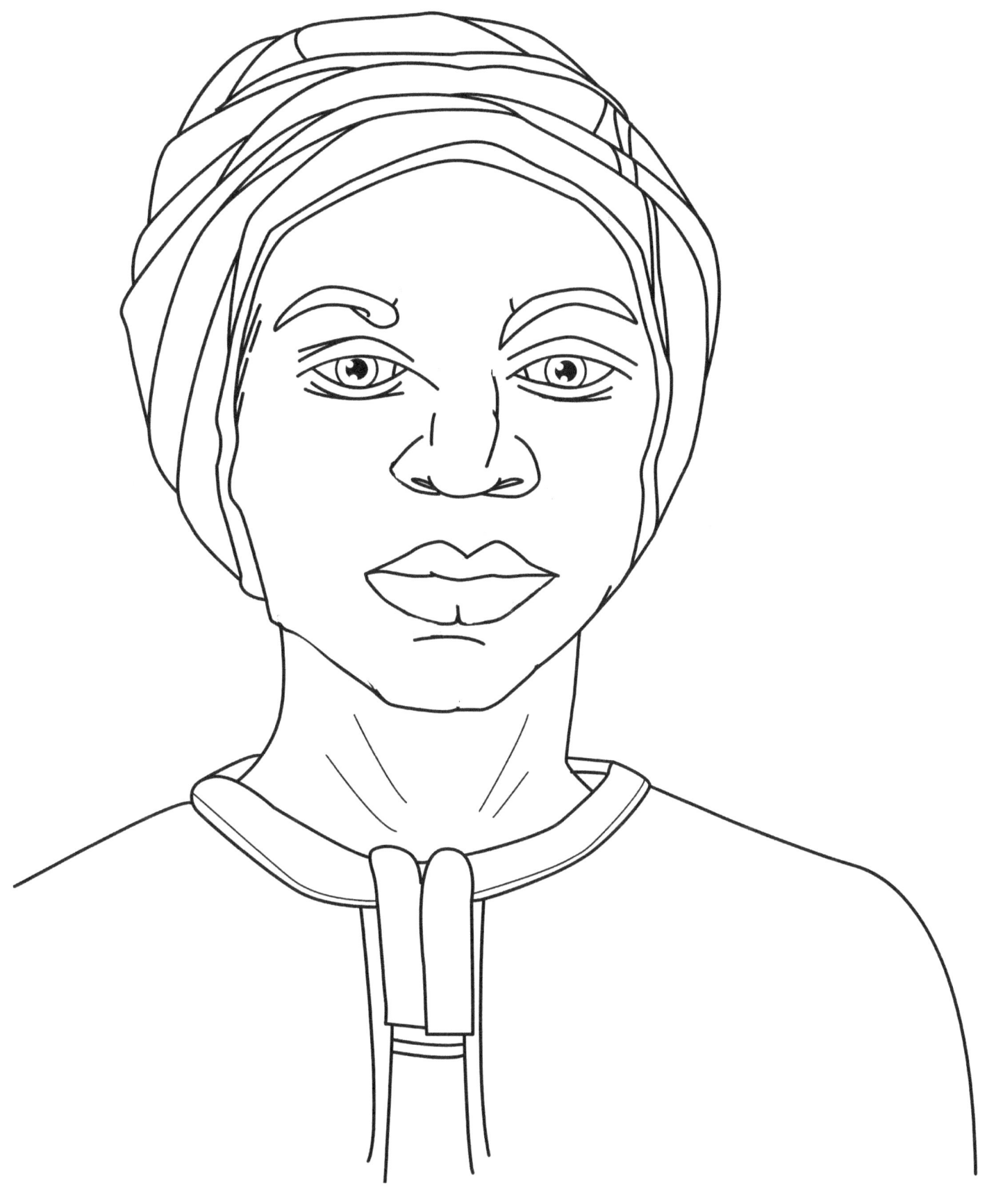

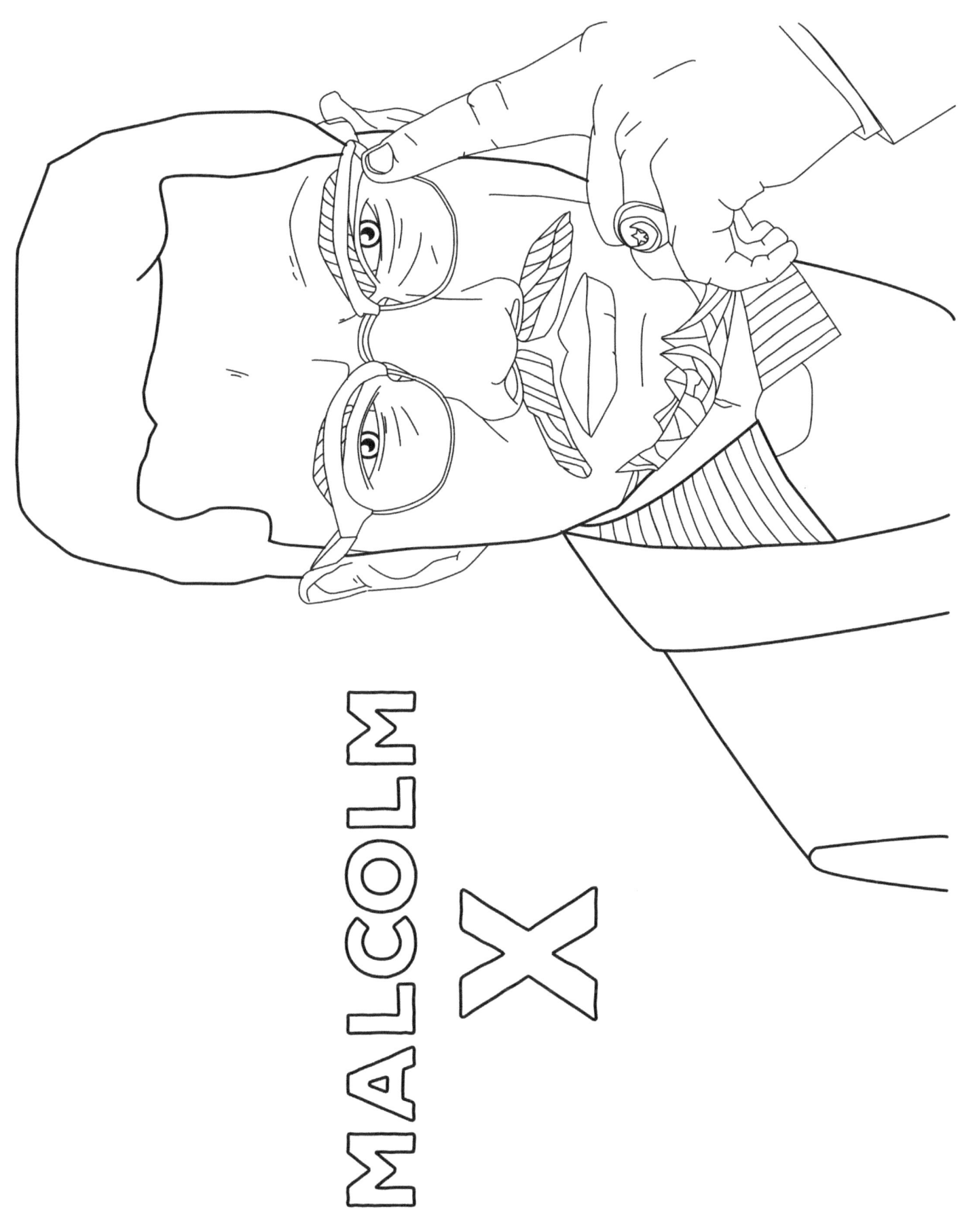

MALCOLM X

PELE

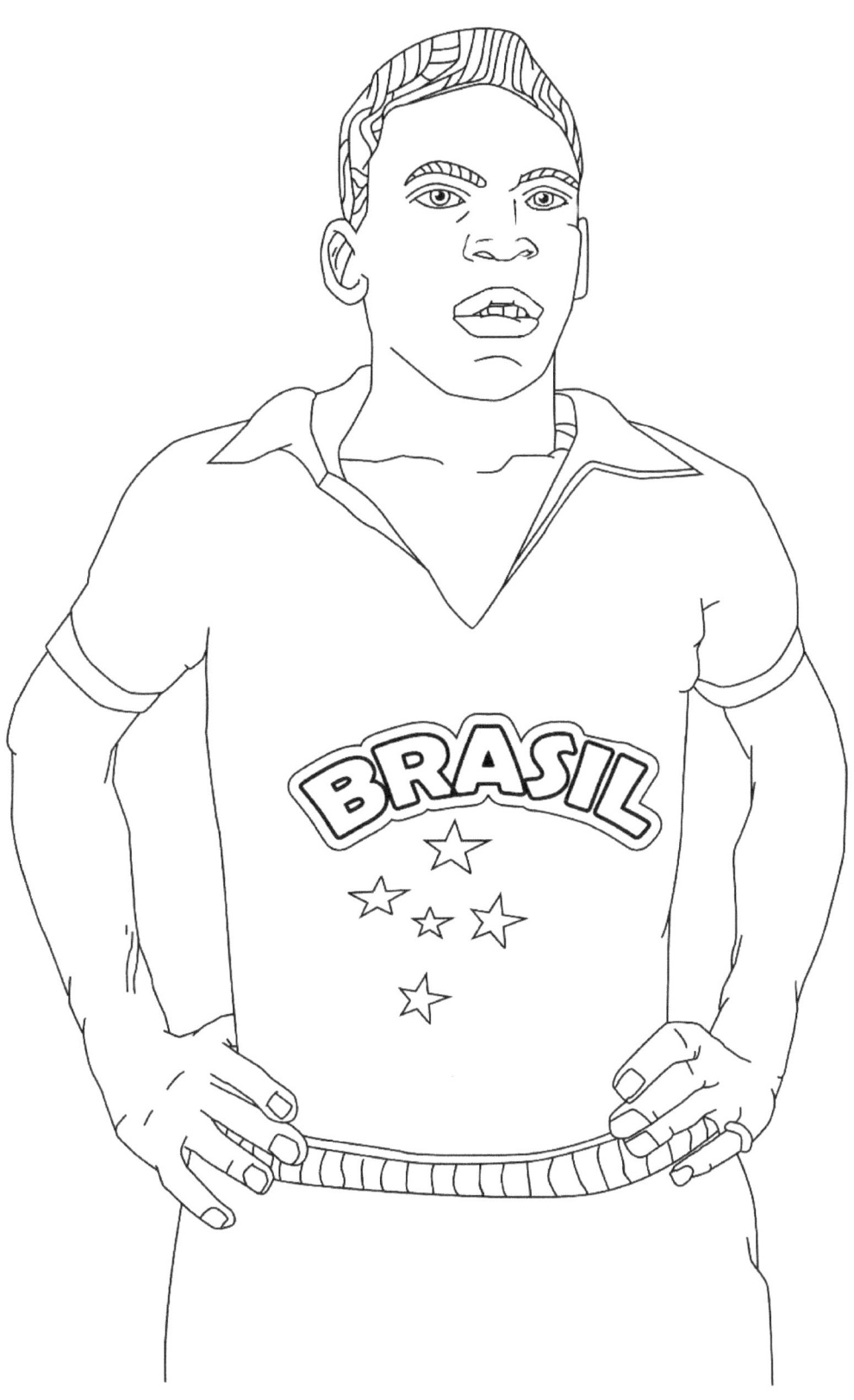

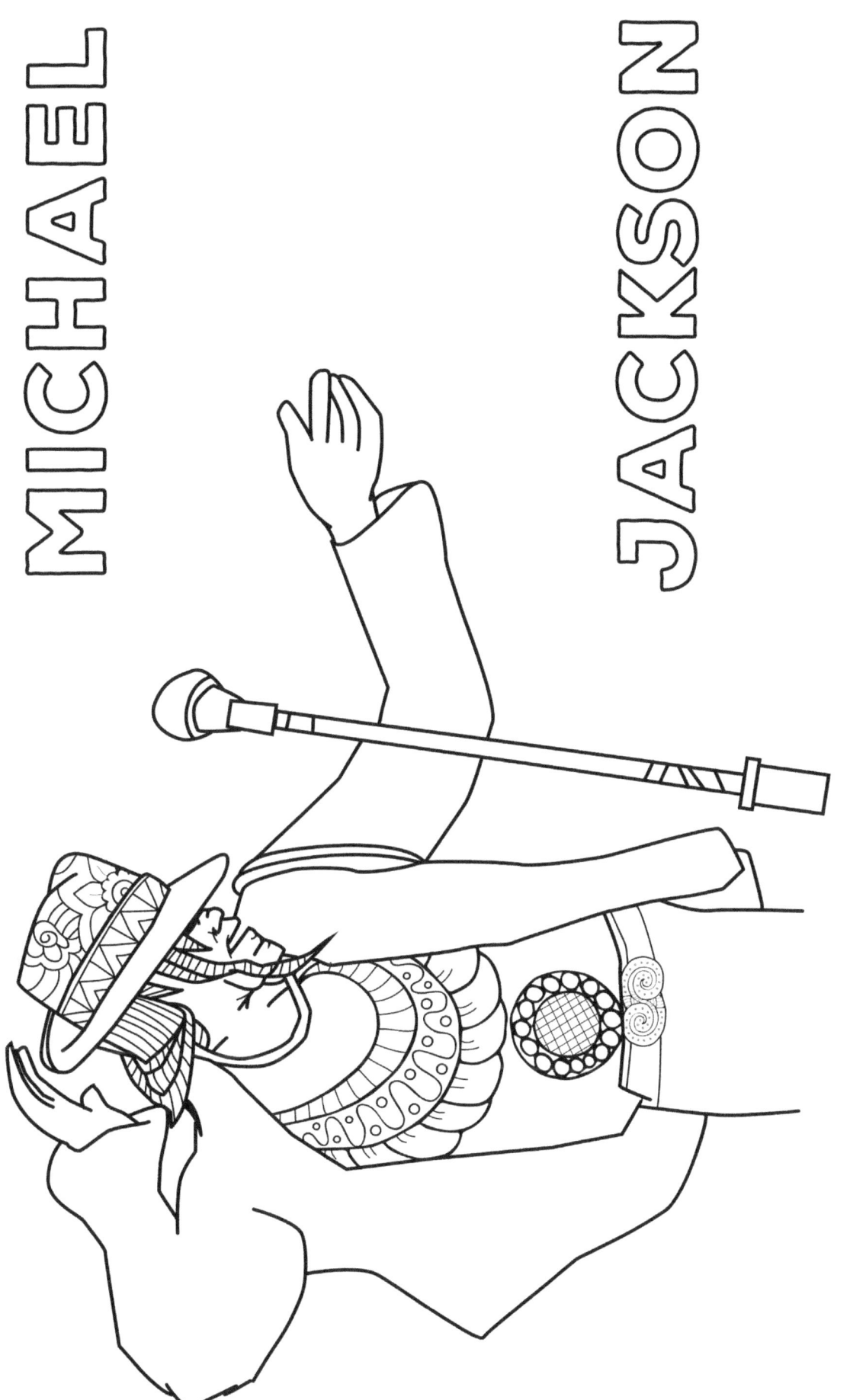

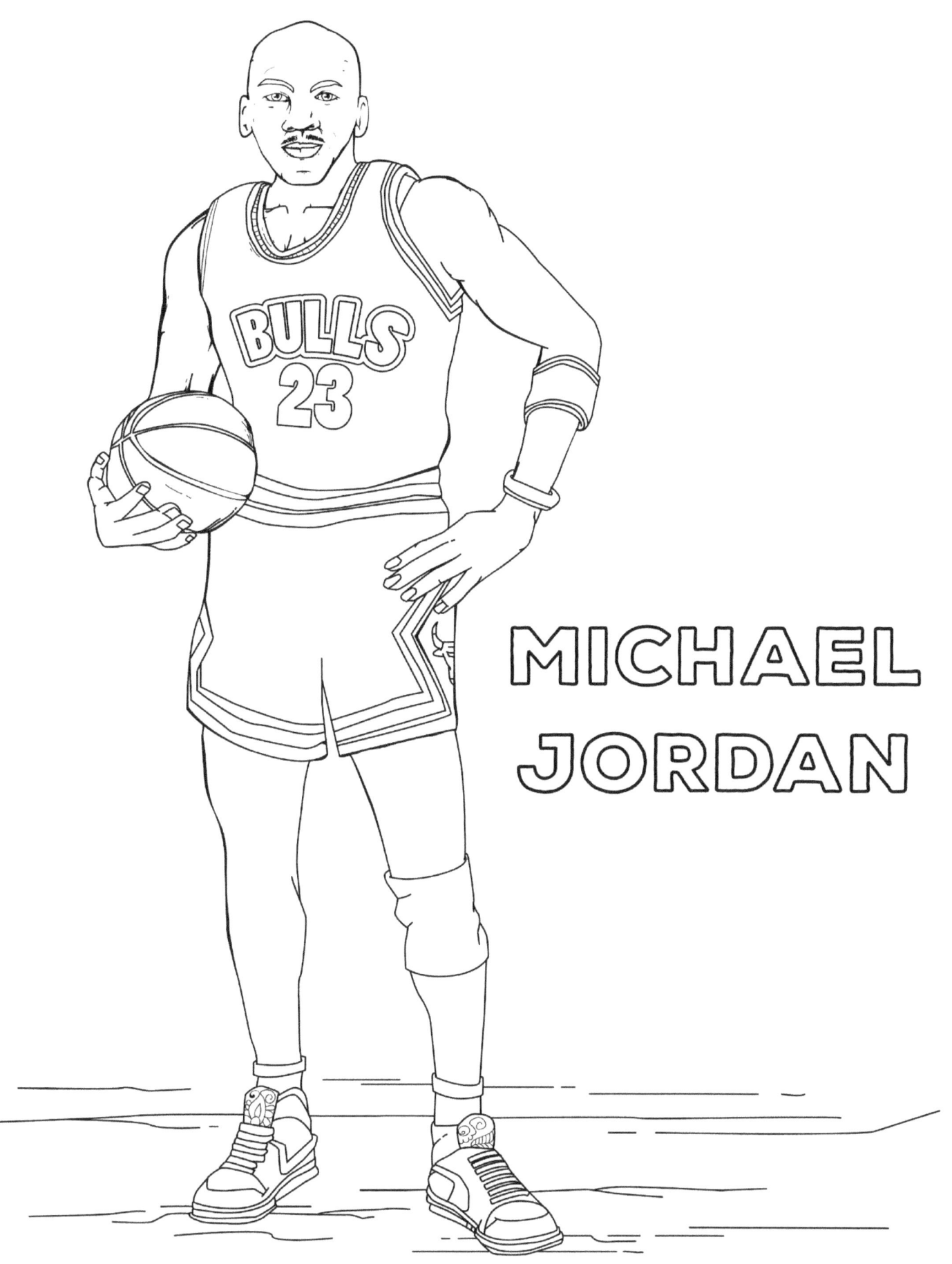

MICHAEL
JORDAN

USAIN BOLT

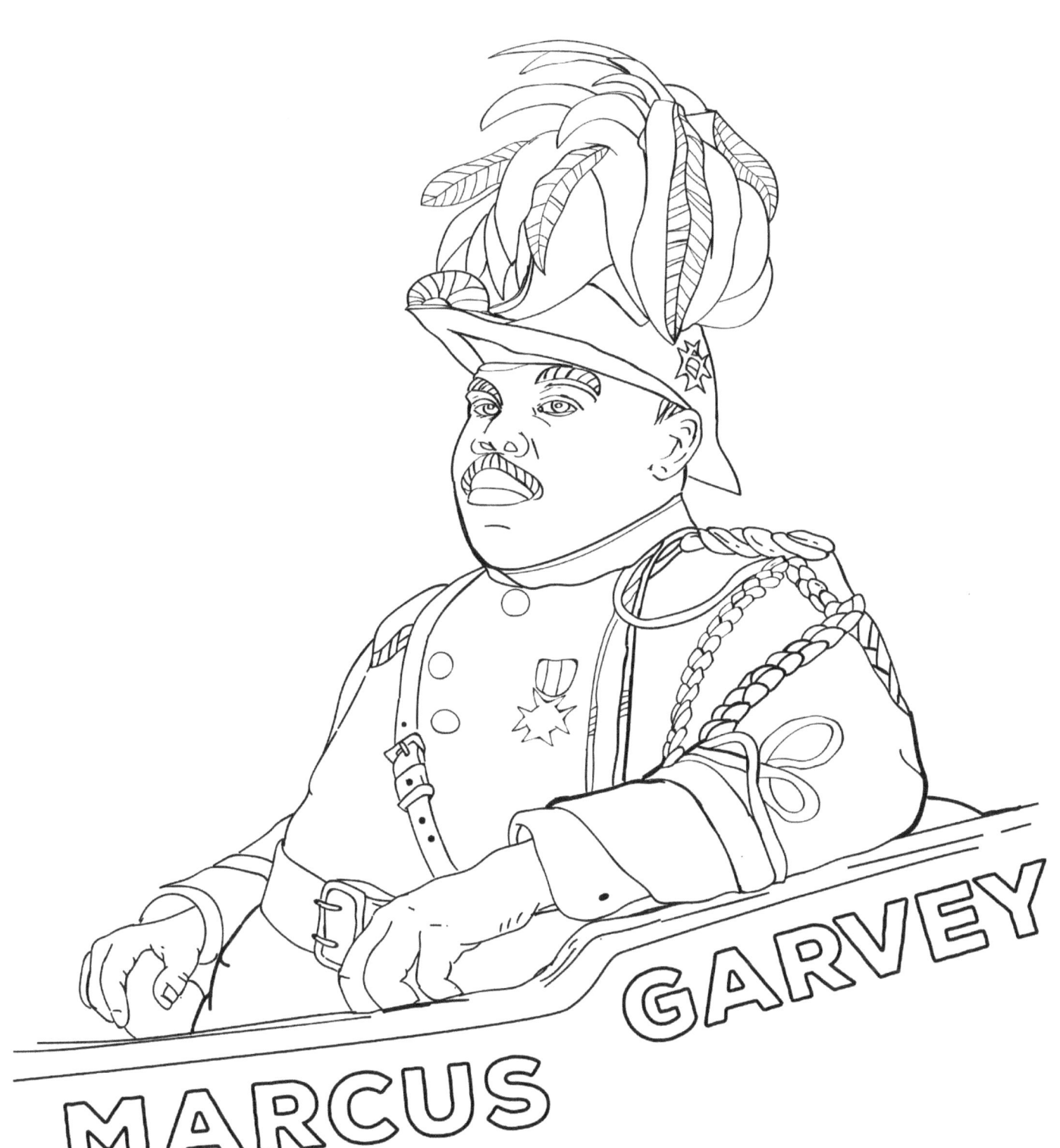

MARCUS GARVEY

HARRIET TUBMAN

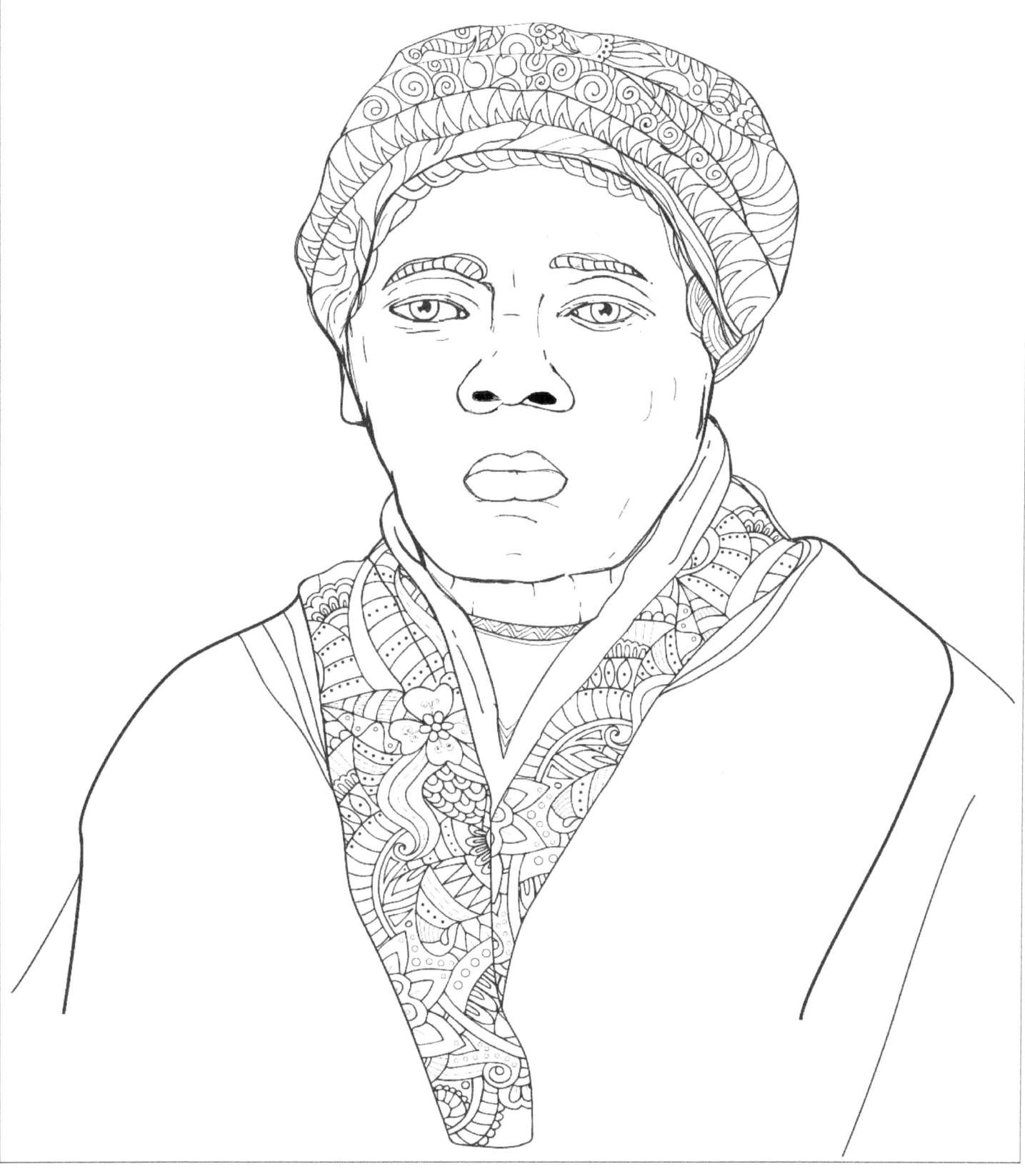

BILLIE HOLIDAY

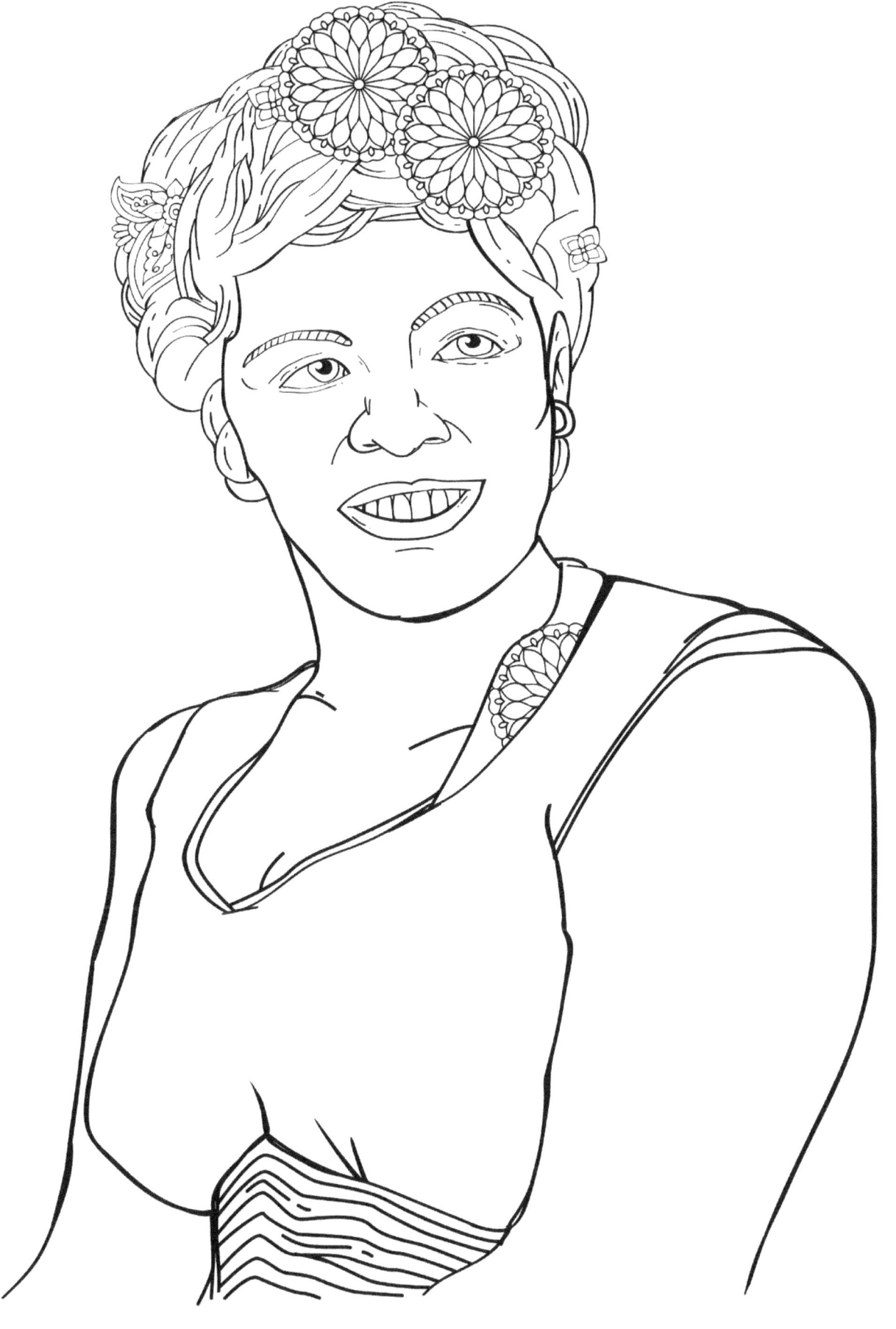

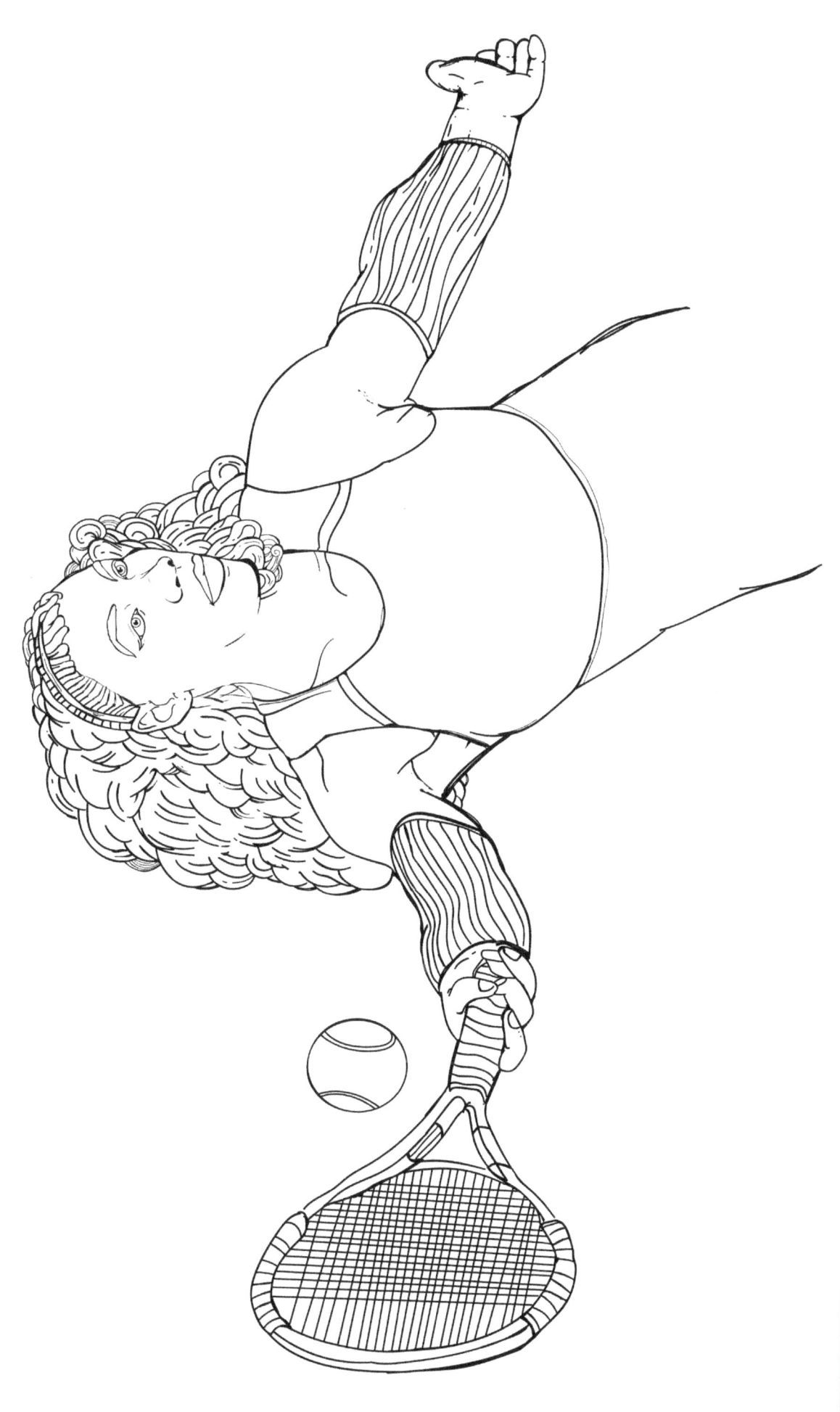

SERENA WILLIAMS

THURGOOD MARSHALL

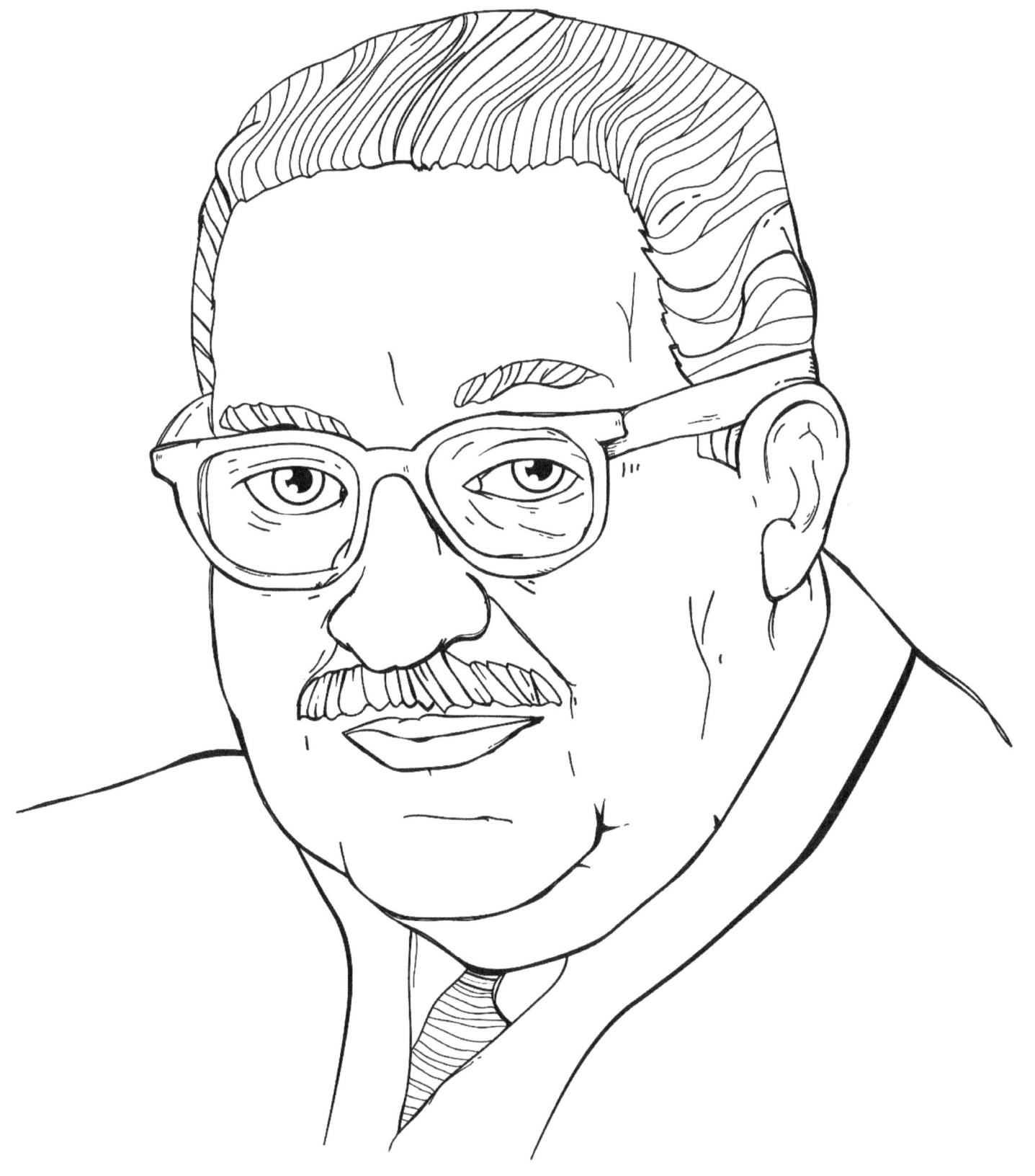

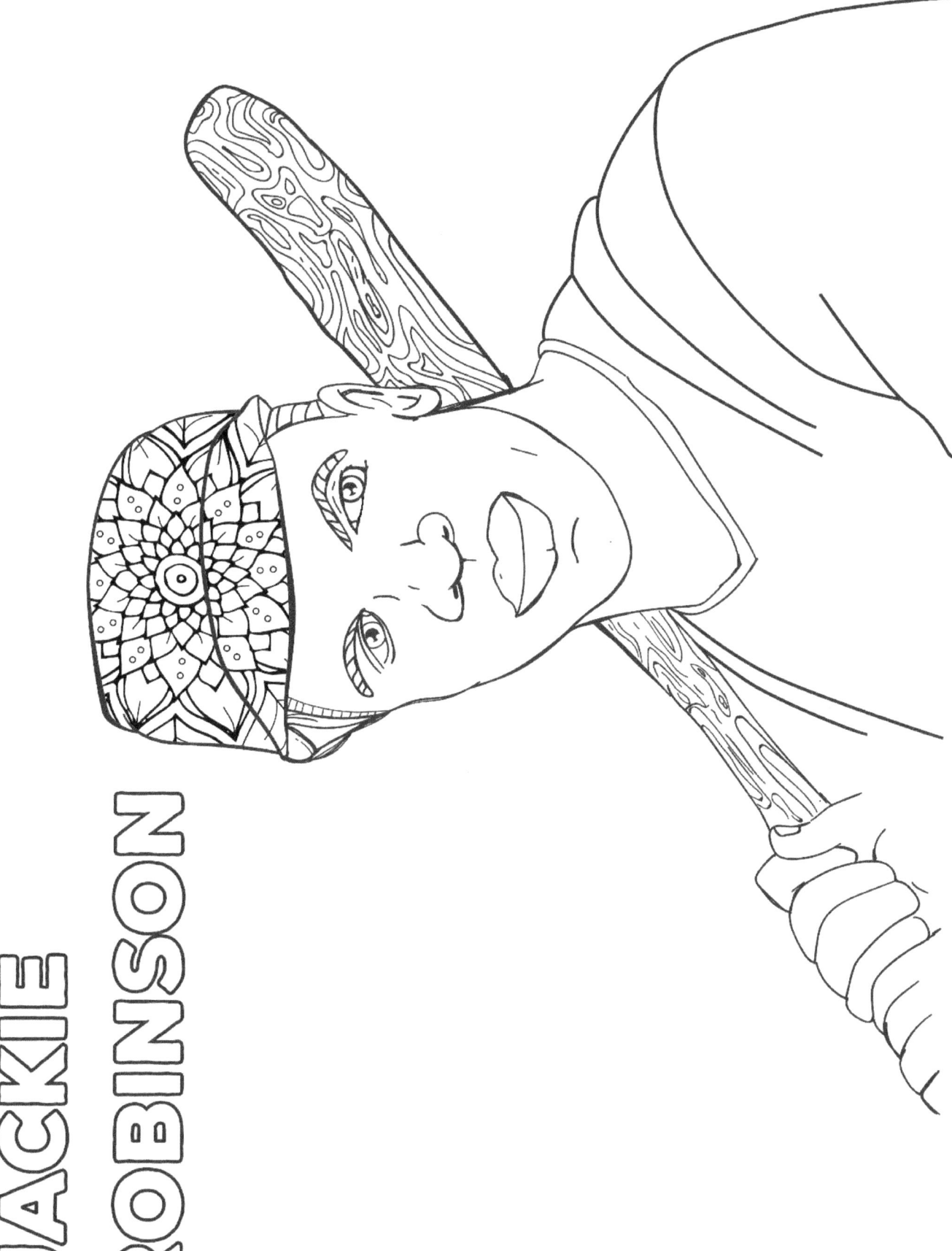

JACKIE ROBINSON

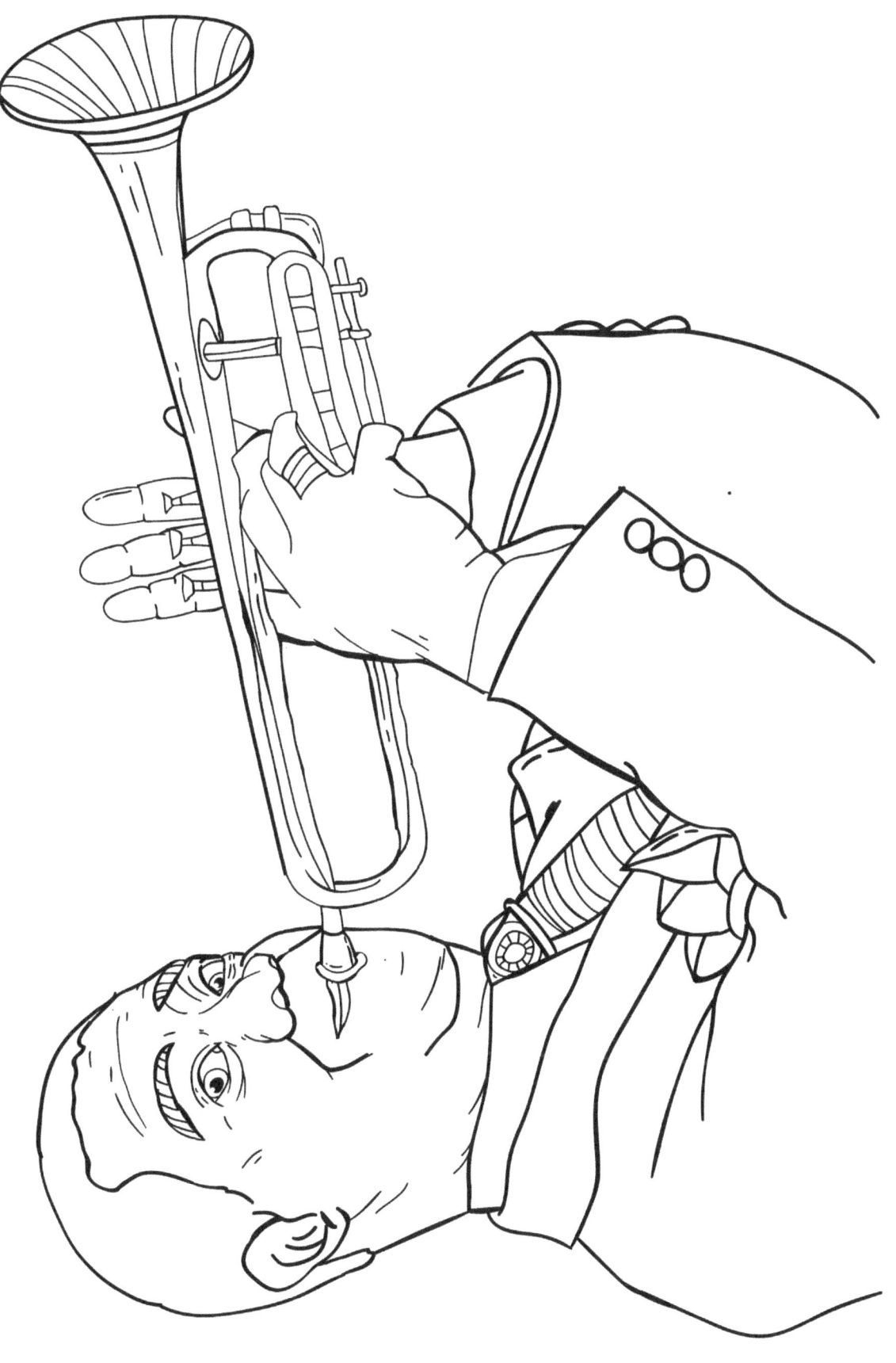

LOUIS ARMSTRONG

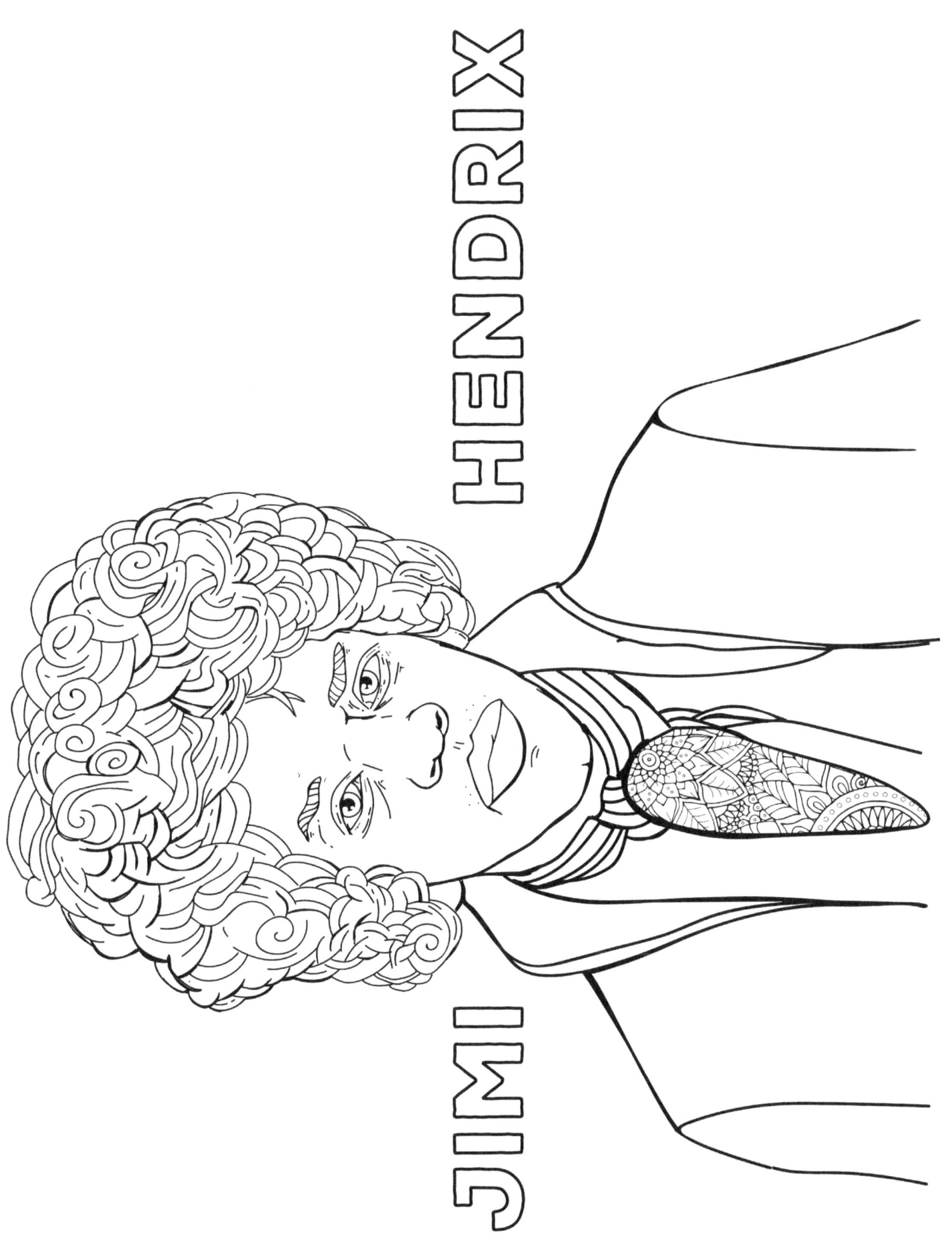

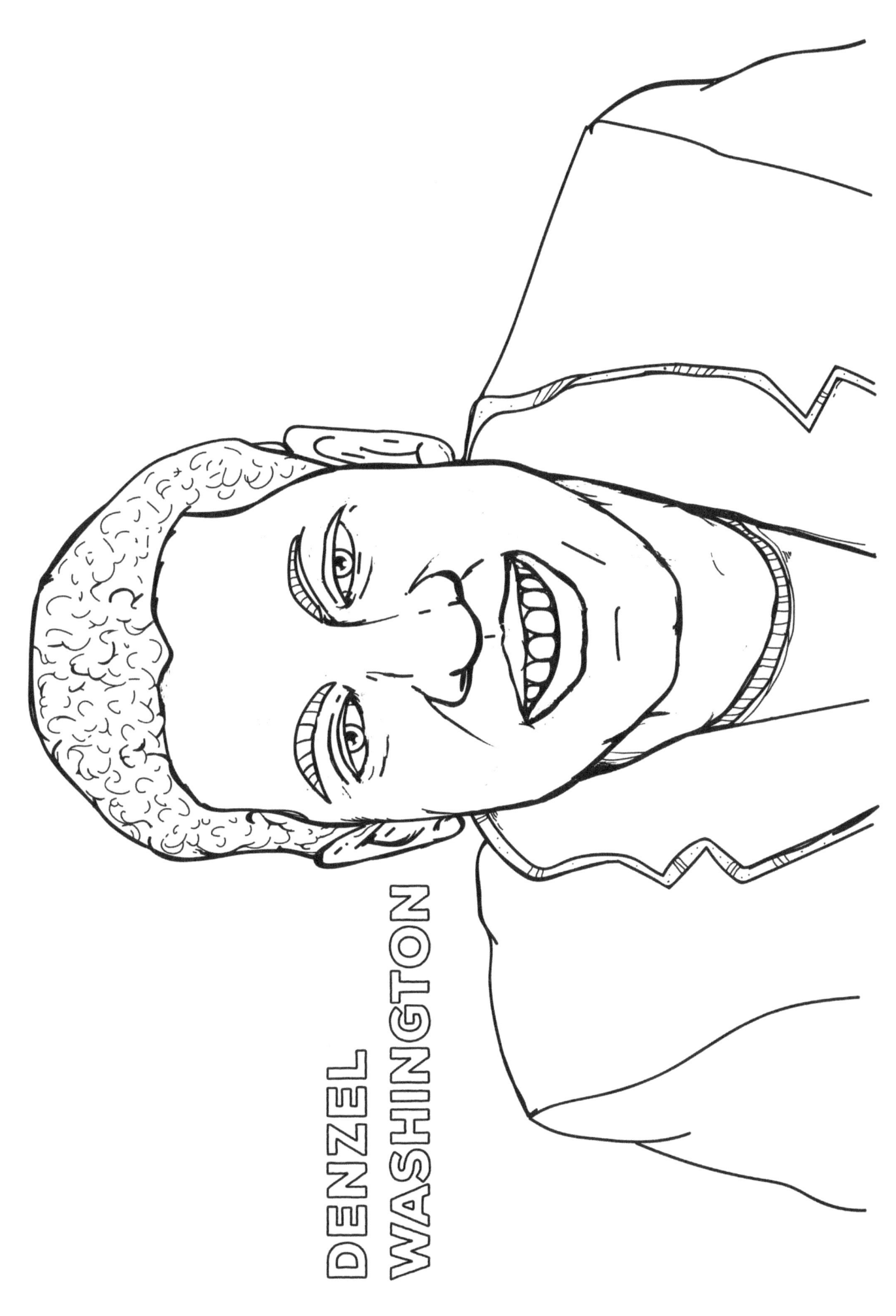

DENZEL
WASHINGTON

Halle Berry

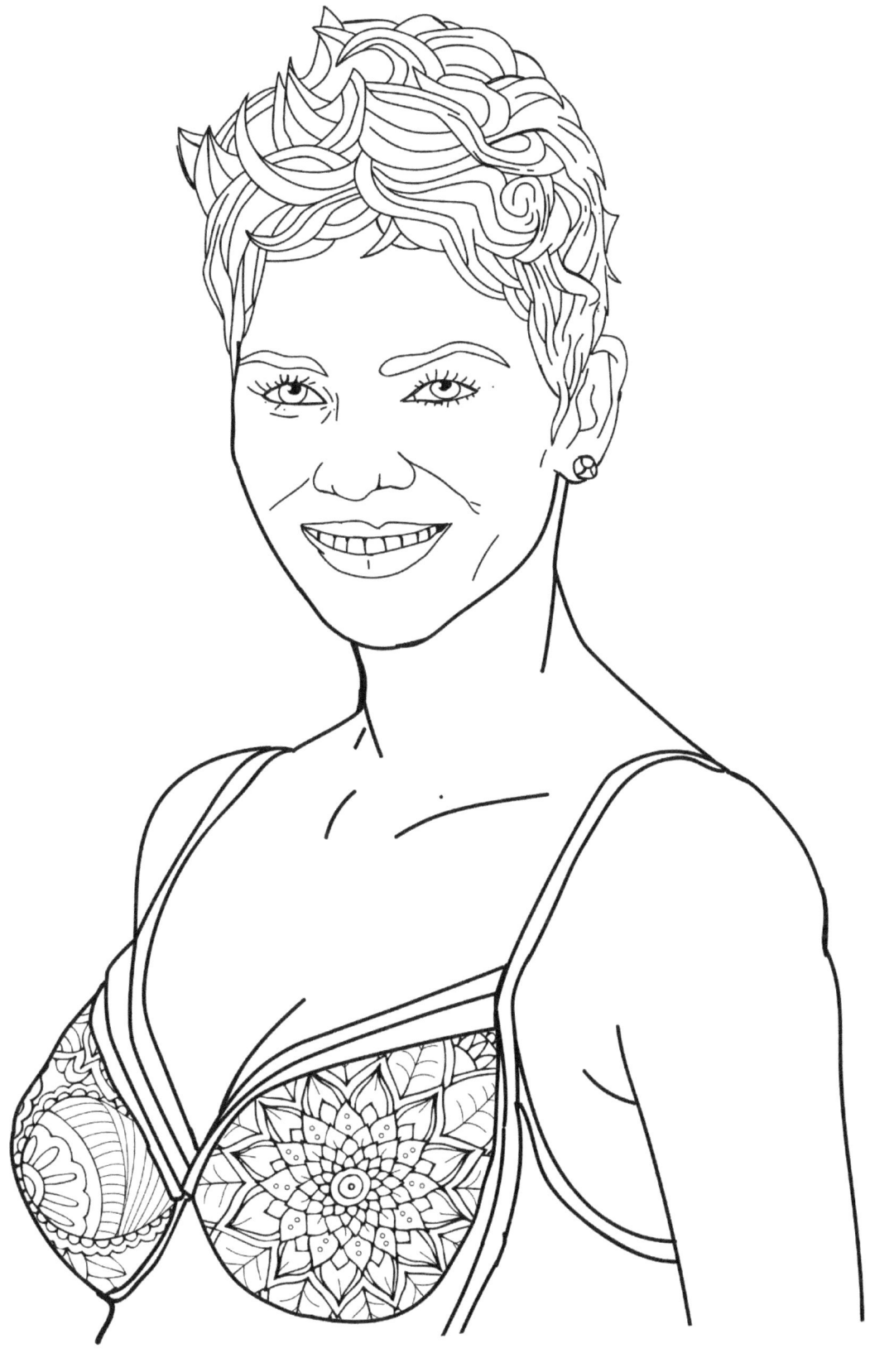

HAILE SELASSIE

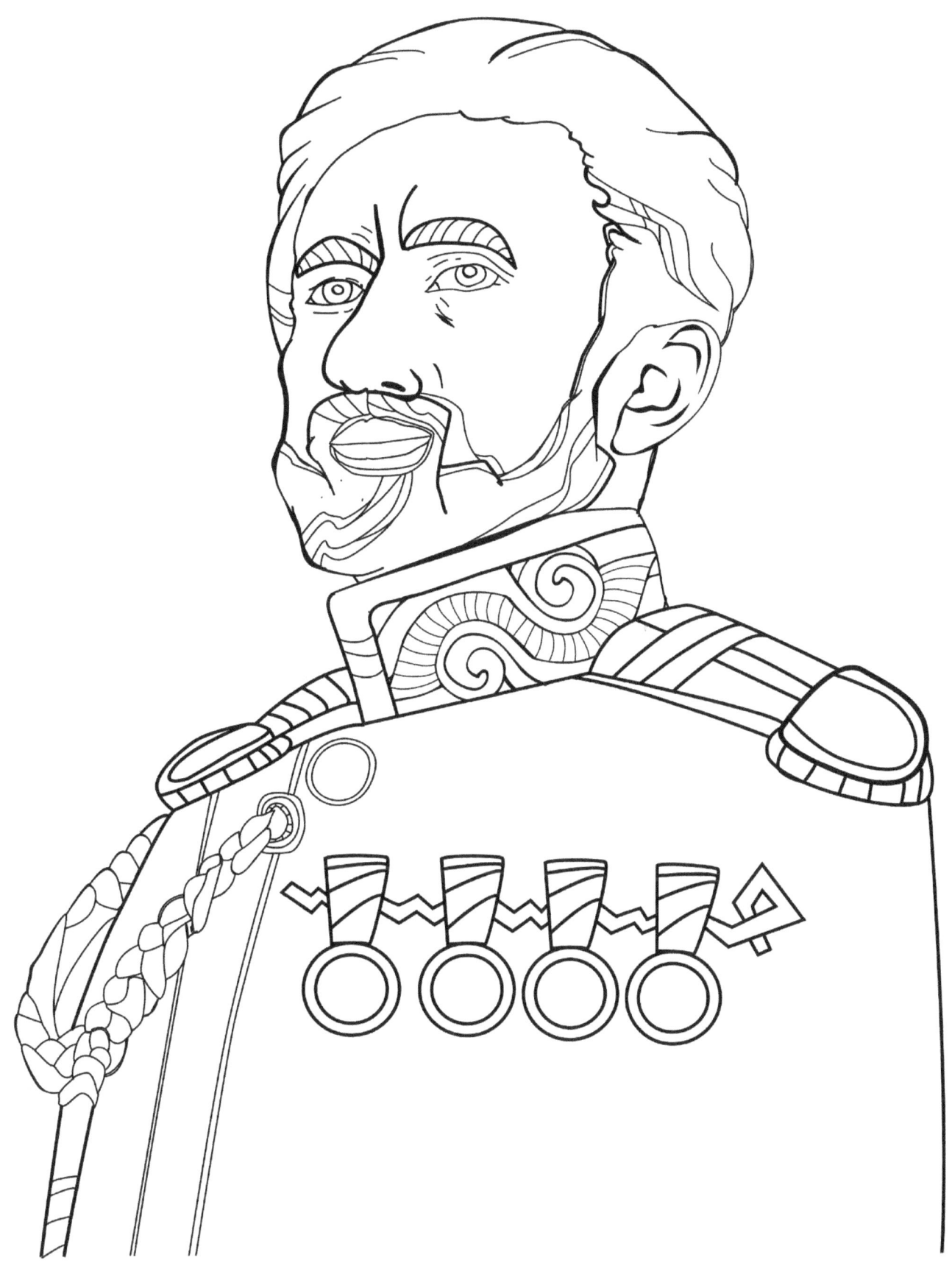

SHAKA
ZULU

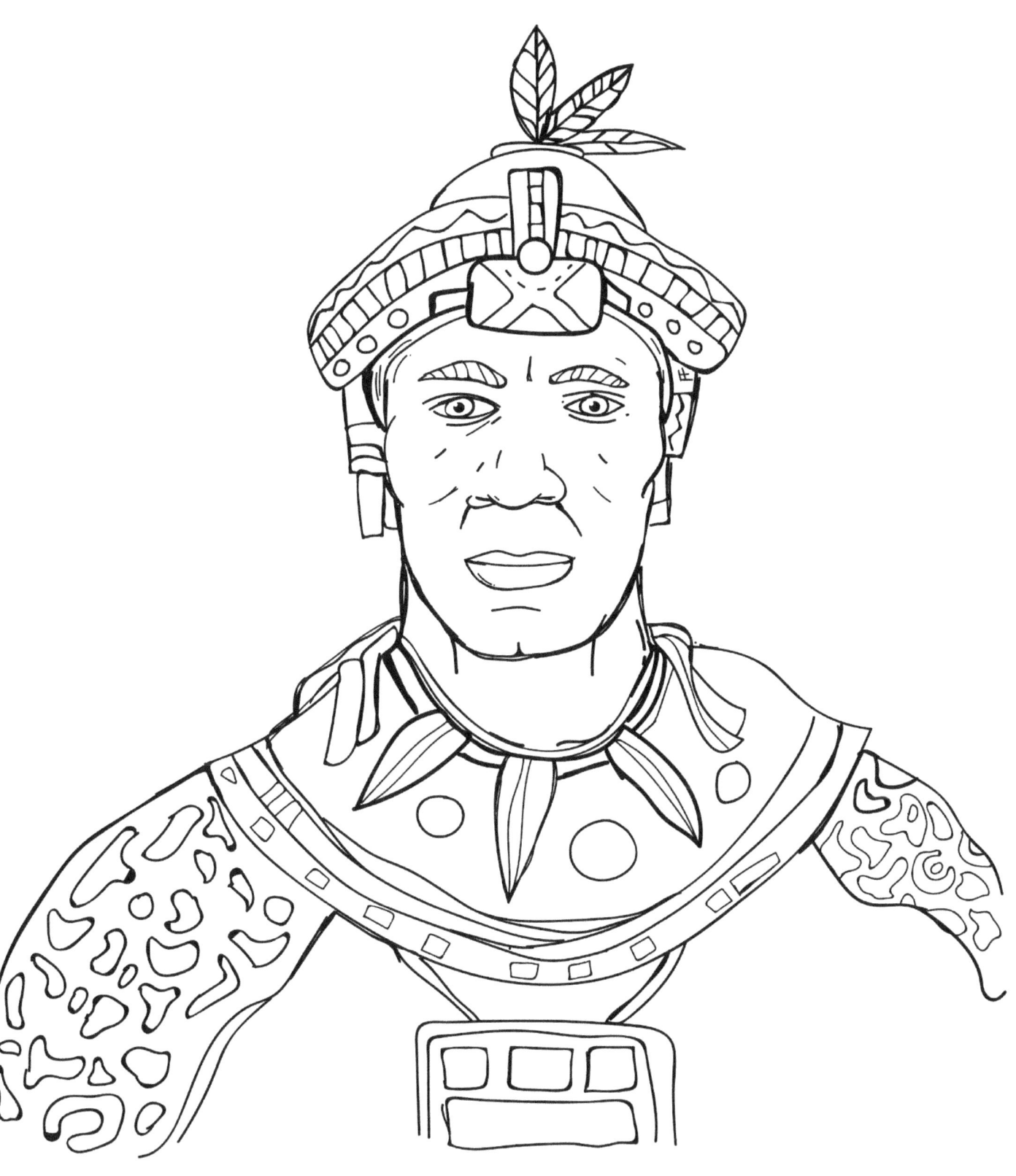

WHOOPI GOLDBERG

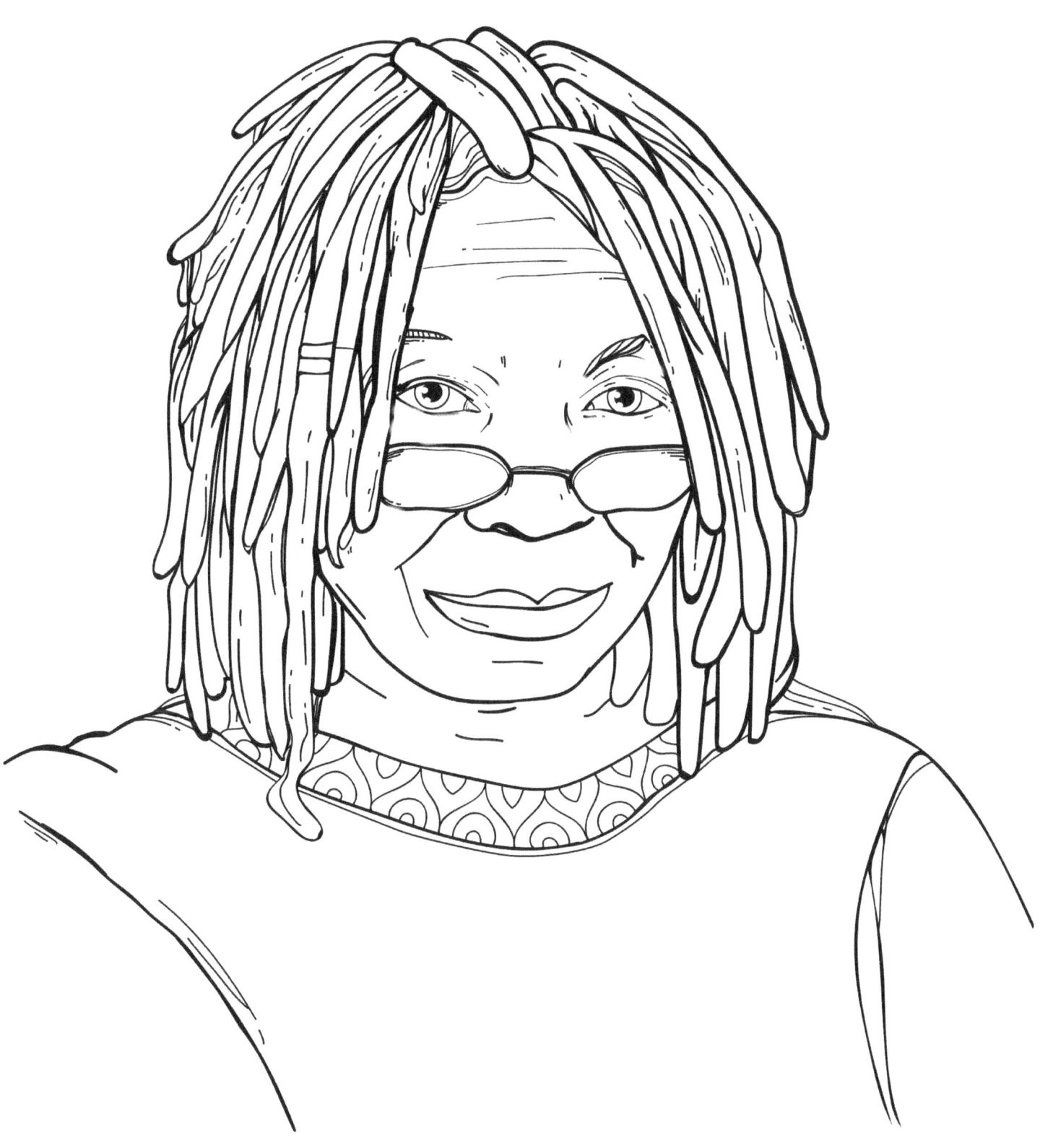

JEAN-MICHEL BASQUIAT

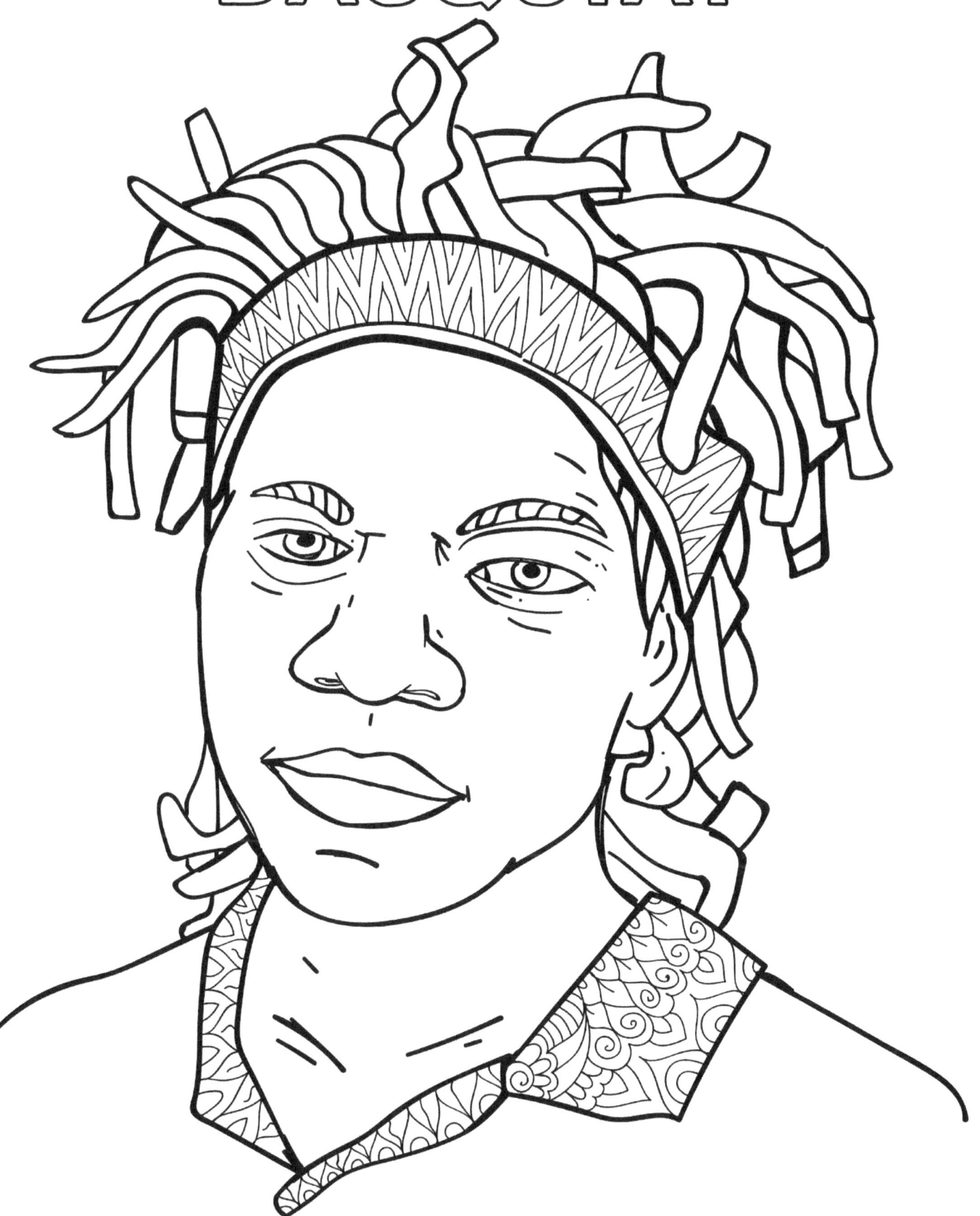

QUINCY JONES

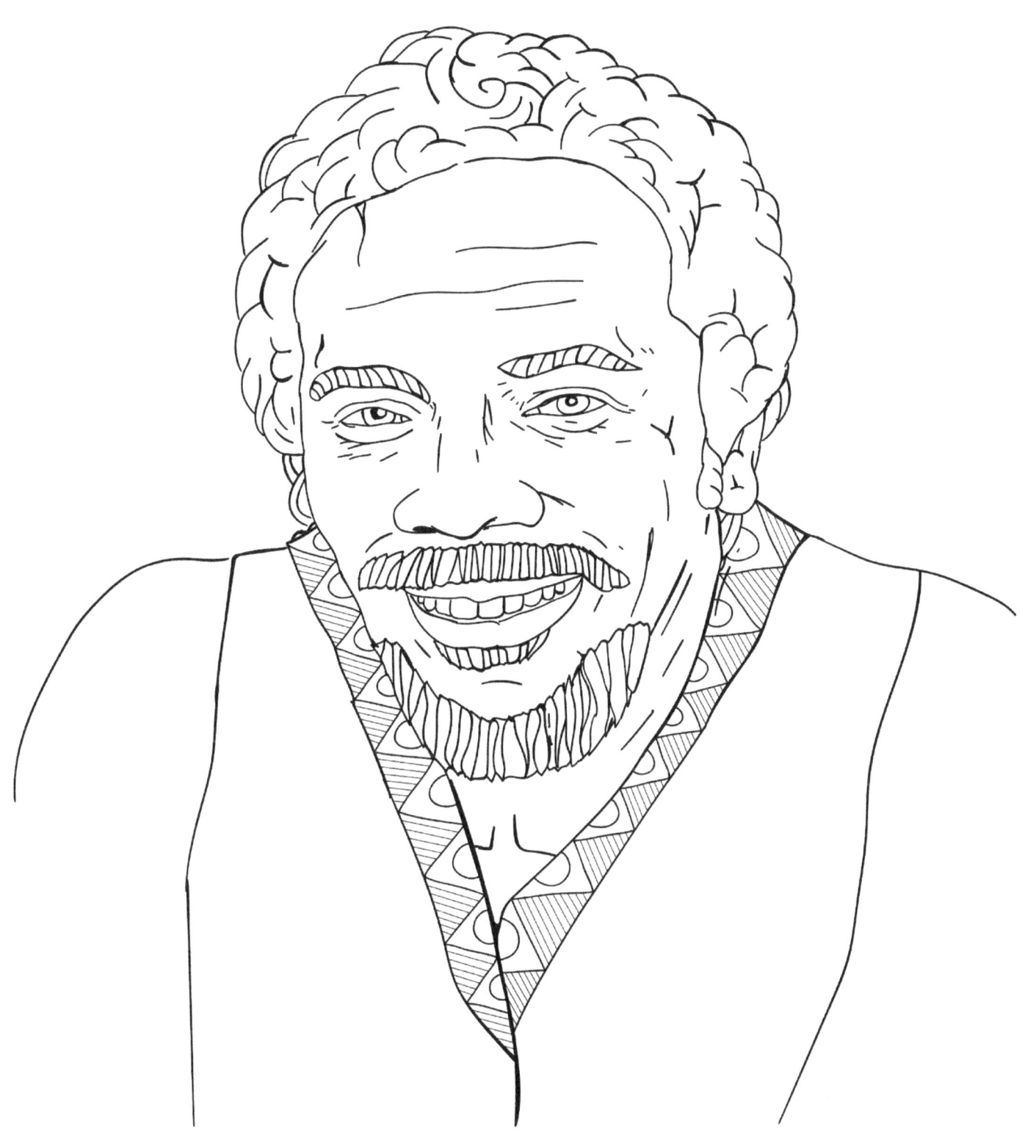

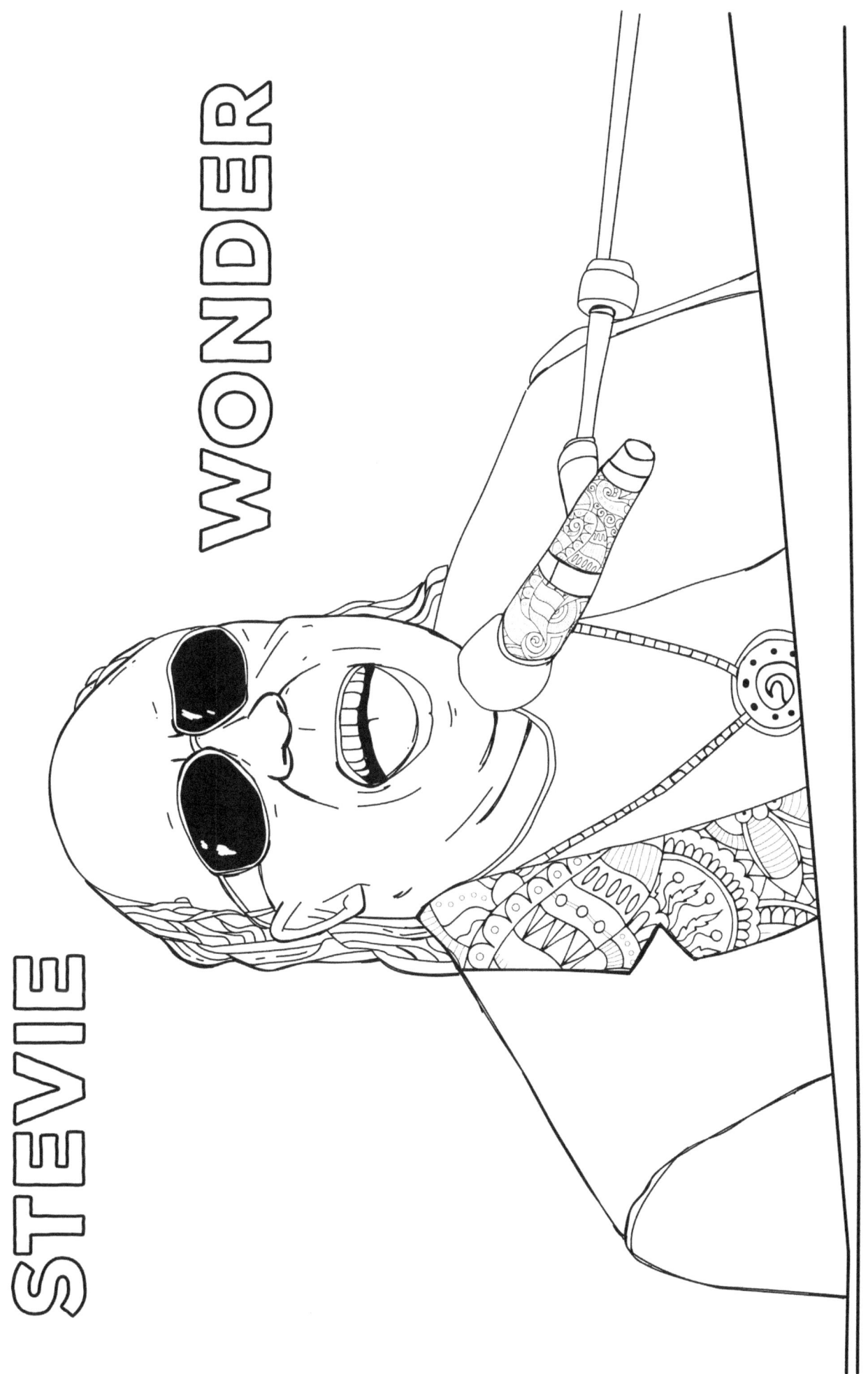

RAY CHARLES

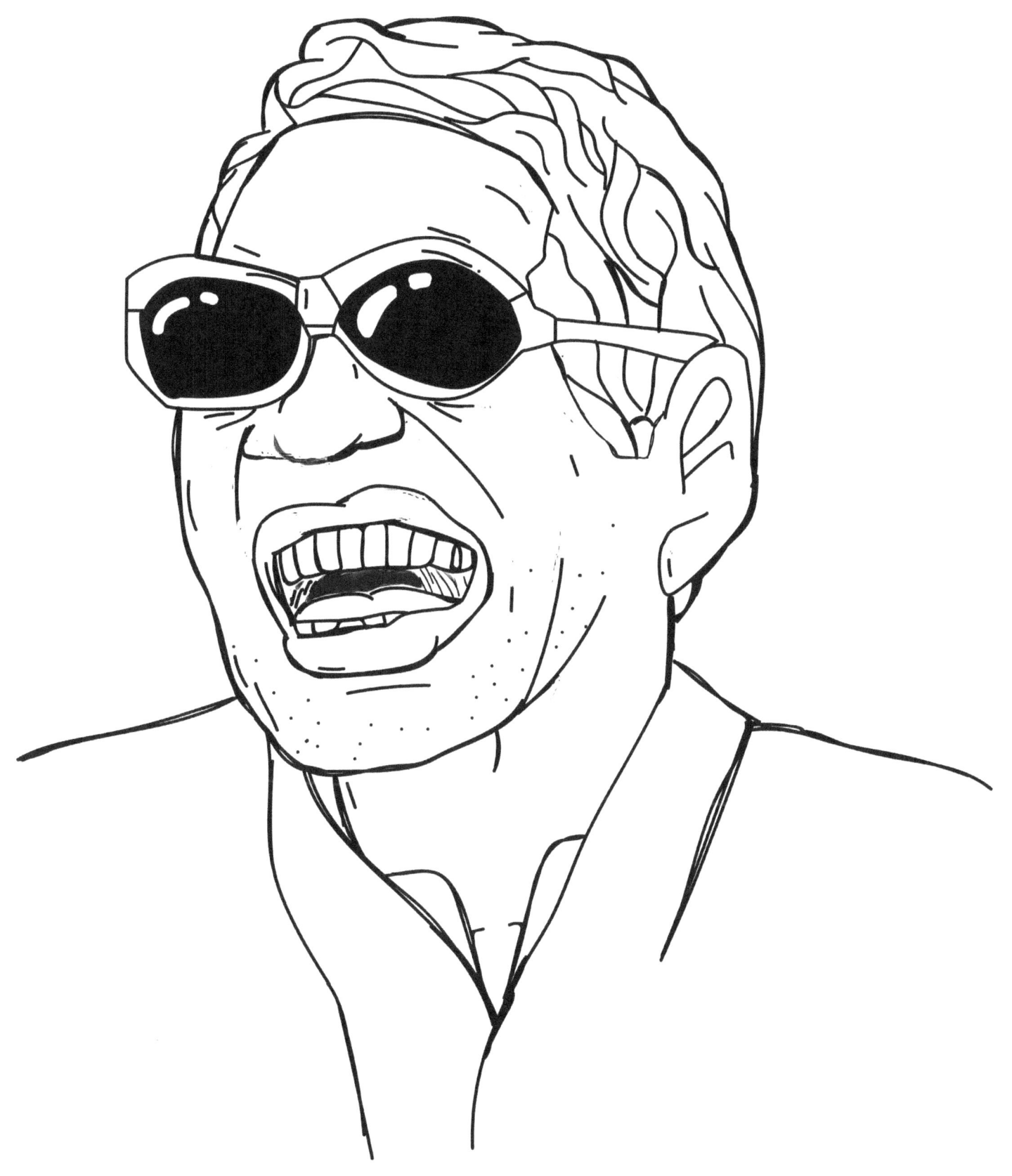

Thank you for purchasing this book.

If you would like to know more about Aryla Publishing Books please visit:-

www.ArylaPublishing.com

Or follow us on
Facebook
Twitter
Instagram
for *free promotions*

@arylapublishing

We would love to know what you think of this book so please leave us a review.

Have a wonderful day ☺

Other Coloring Books from Aryla Publishing

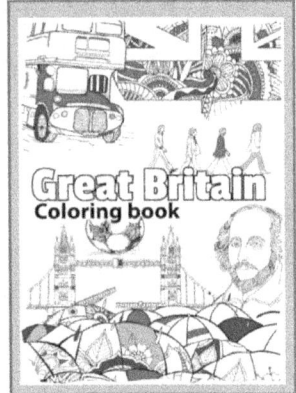
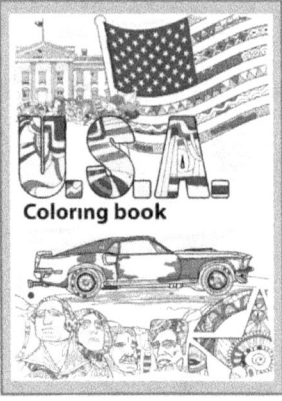
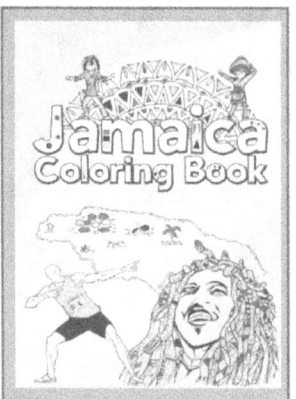
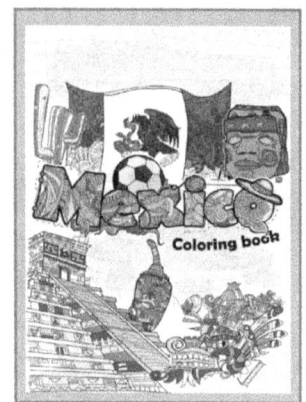

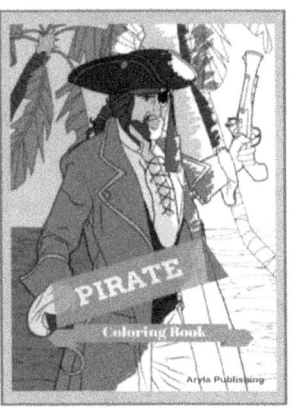
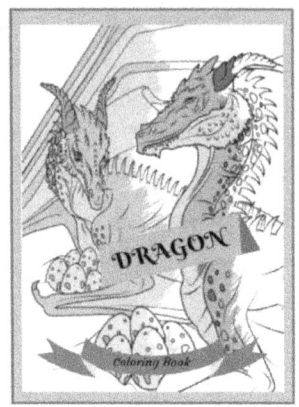
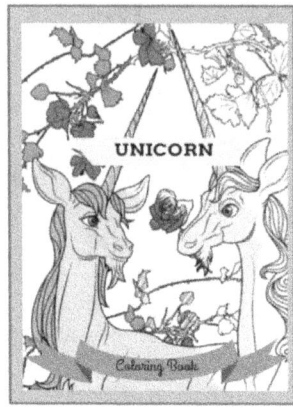
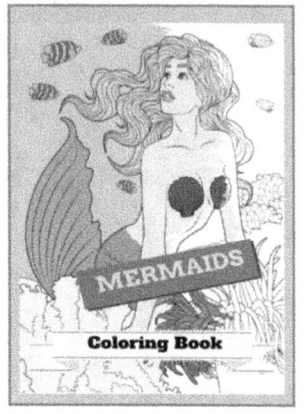

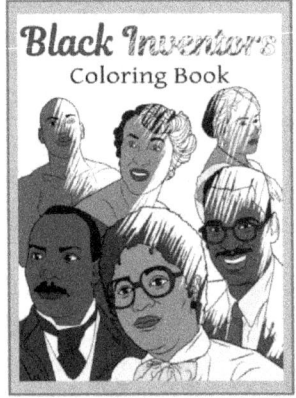
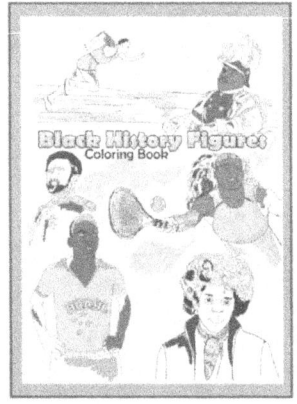
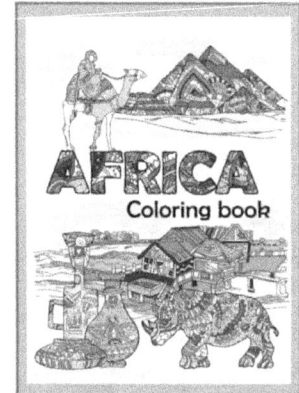
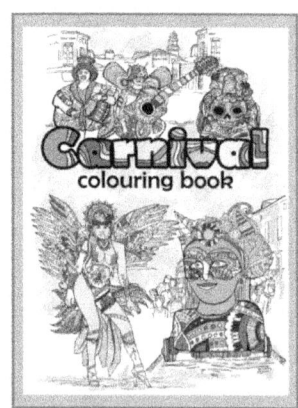

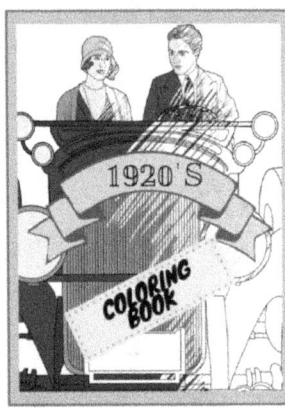
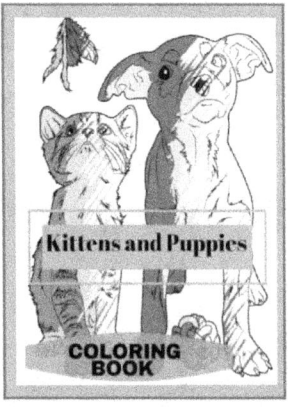
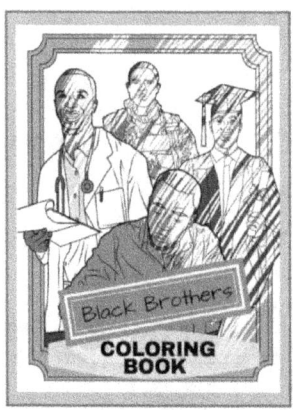
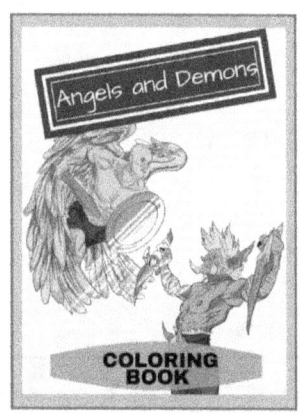

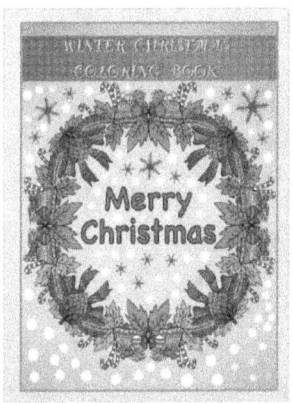
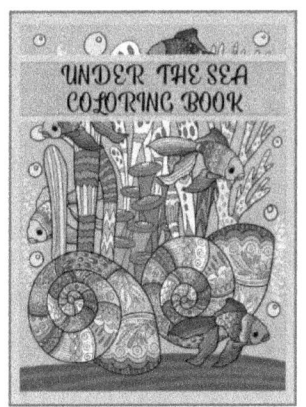
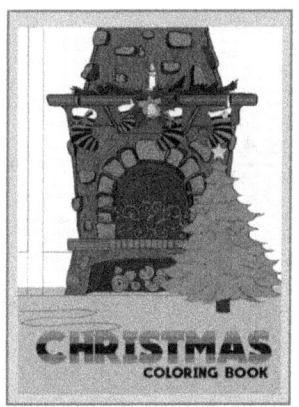
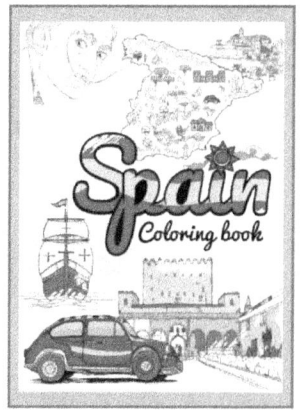
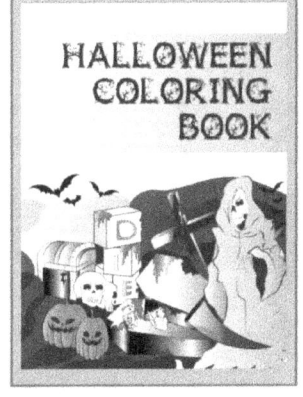
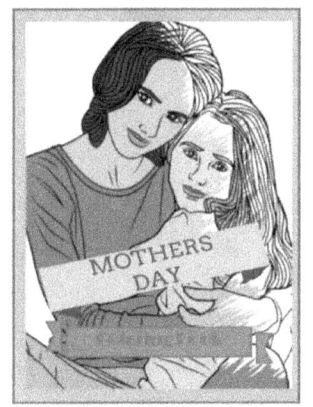
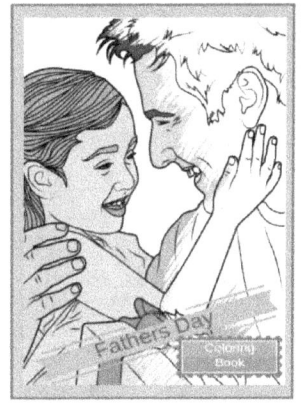
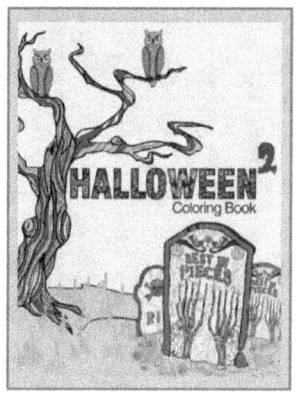
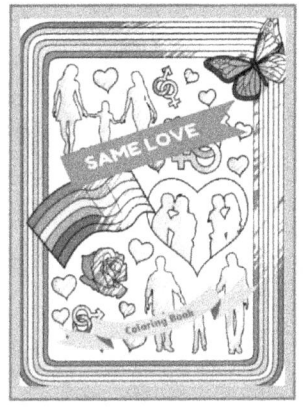
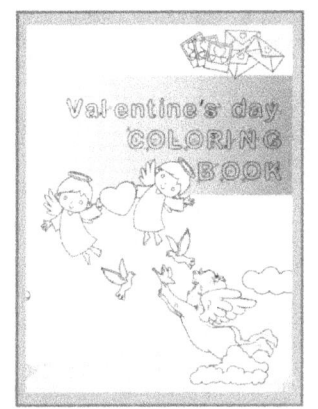
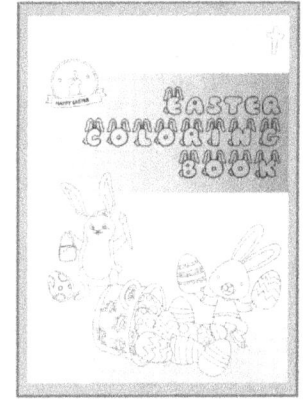
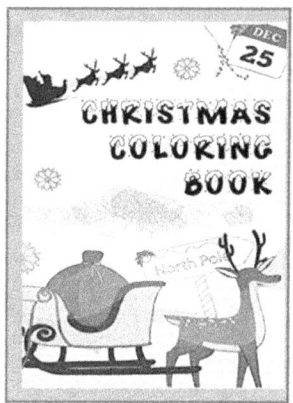
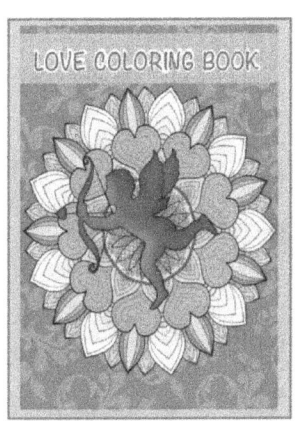
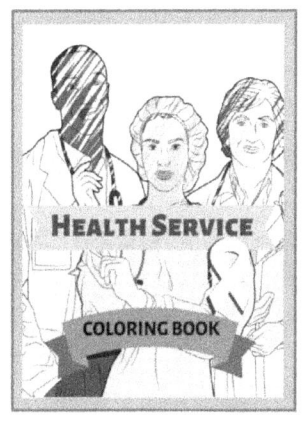
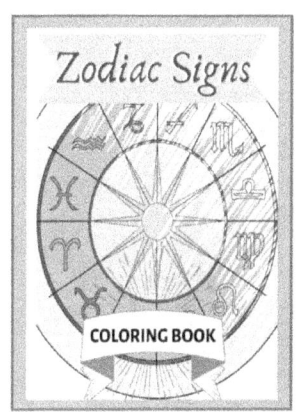
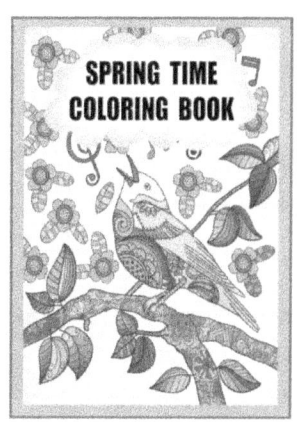

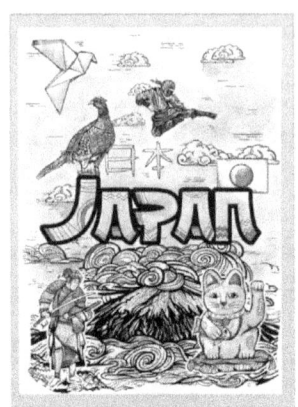

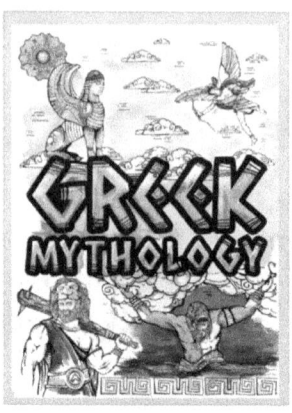

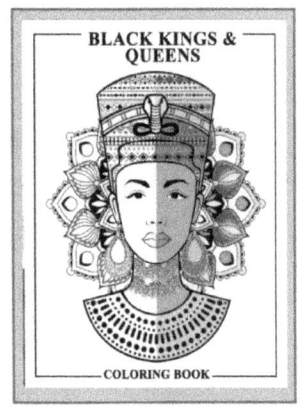

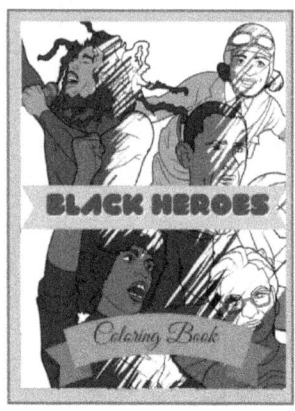

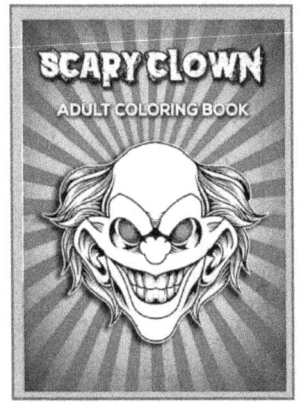

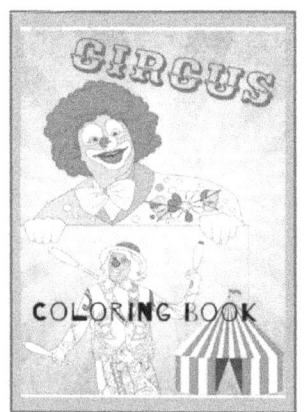

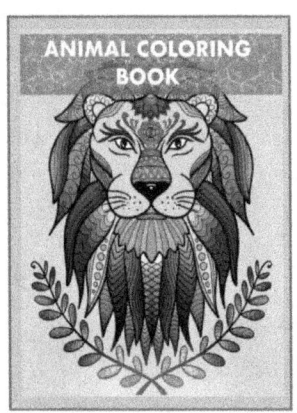

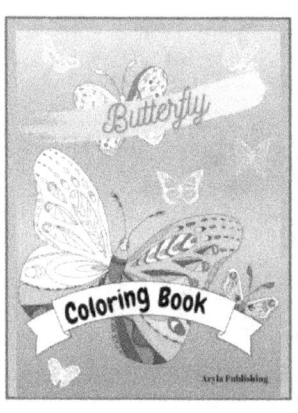

Color In Fun
Kids Books

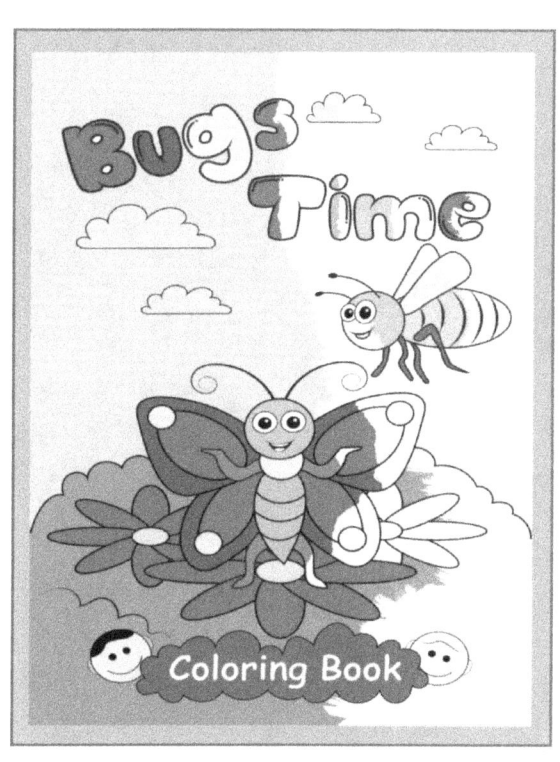

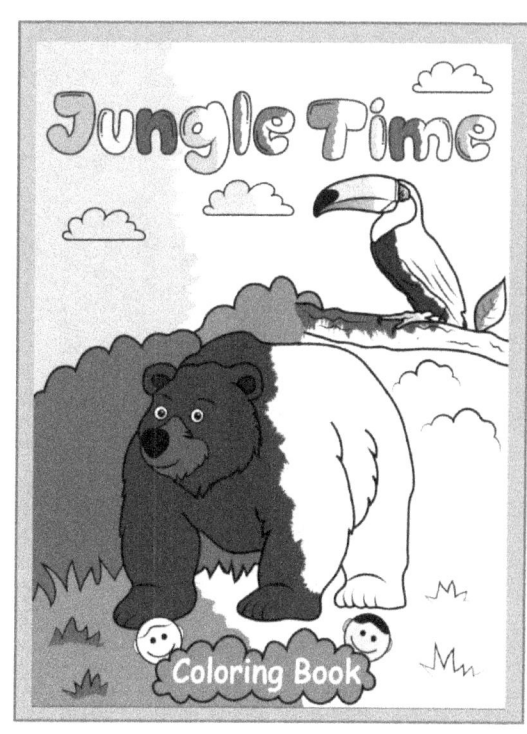

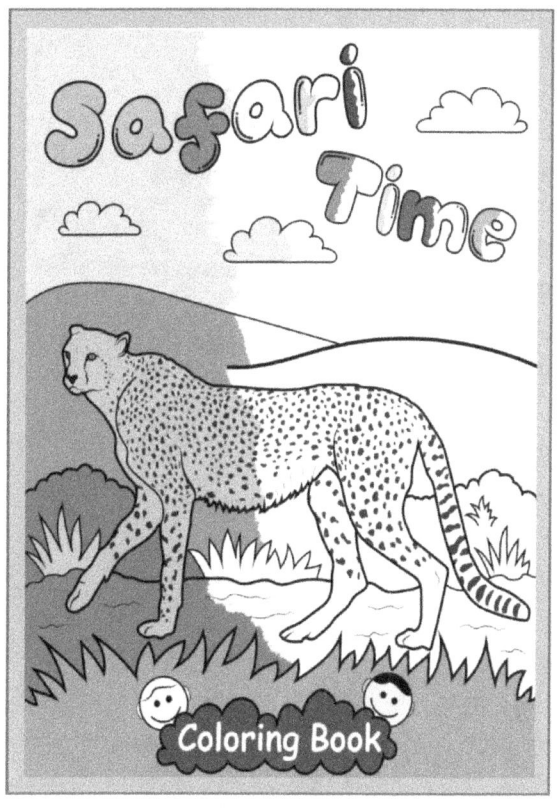

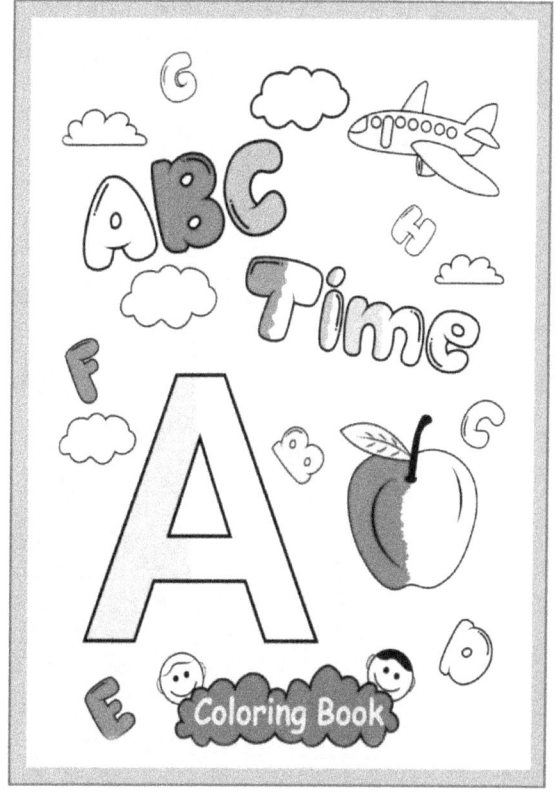

Visit **www.ArylaPublishing.com**
to find out about all new releases.

Follow us @arylapublishing on Twitter Instagram & Facebook

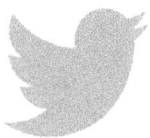  

Search for Aryla Publishing on

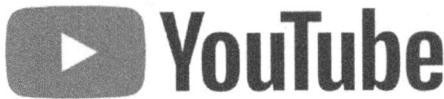 YouTube

Check out our <u>Book Trailers</u>

<u>*Subscribe*</u> *to keep up to date with new releases!*